W9-AXB-139

LP 248.4 OST
Osteen, Victoria.
Love your life : living happy,
healthy, and whole /

PALM BEACH COUNTY
LIBRARY SYSTEM
3650 SUMMIT BLVD.
WEST PALM BEACH, FLORIDA 33406

LOVE YOUR LIFE

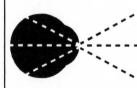 This Large Print Book carries the
Seal of Approval of N.A.V.H.

LOVE YOUR LIFE

LIVING HAPPY, HEALTHY, AND WHOLE

VICTORIA OSTEEN

THORNDIKE PRESS

A part of Gale, Cengage Learning

GALE
CENGAGE Learning

Detroit • New York • San Francisco • New Haven, Conn • Waterville, Maine • London

GALE
CENGAGE Learning

Copyright © 2008 by Victoria Osteen.
Thorndike Press, a part of Gale, Cengage Learning.

ALL RIGHTS RESERVED
The names of all persons other than family members and public figures mentioned in this book are pseudonyms.
Thorndike Press® Large Print Inspirational.
The text of this Large Print edition is unabridged.
Other aspects of the book may vary from the original edition.
Set in 16 pt. Plantin.
Printed on permanent paper.

LIBRARY OF CONGRESS CATALOGING-IN-PUBLICATION DATA

Osteen, Victoria.
    Love your life : living happy, healthy, and whole / by Victoria Osteen. — Large print ed.
       p. cm.
    Includes bibliographical references.
    ISBN-13 978-1-4104-1469-4 (hardcover : alk. paper)
    ISBN-10 1-4104-1469-8 (hardcover : alk. paper)
    ISBN-13 978-1-59415-285-6 (softcover : alk. paper)
    ISBN-10 1-59415-285-3 (softcover : alk. paper)
    1. Christian women—Religious life. 2. Self realization—Religious aspects—Christianity. 3. Large type books. I. Title.
BV4527.O87 2009
248.4—dc22
                                           2008053448

Published in 2009 by arrangement with Free Press, a division of Simon & Schuster, Inc.

Printed in the United States of America
1 2 3 4 5 6 7 13 12 11 10 09

To Joel, my husband and my hero:

I find more reasons to love you every single day, and I am so blessed to be your wife. Thank you for believing in me and encouraging me daily. You challenge me to come up higher and to see the best in every situation, and I truly am a better person because of your love. You are my best friend and my knight in shining armor. I will always love you.

To Jonathan and Alexandra, my beautiful children:

Your smiles light up my world. You have enriched my life beyond measure, and I cherish you both so much. You are my inspiration and my most precious possessions. You are my daily dose of joy, filling my life with love, laughter, and fun. I thank God for you every day, and I love you both with all of my heart.

ACKNOWLEDGMENTS

The experience of writing this book has stretched me and helped me to grow in so many ways. The truth is, though, it is only through God's grace and the people He put in my life that this book became a reality. There are so many people who helped me and to whom I owe my appreciation and gratitude.

First, I want to thank Carolyn Reidy, Dominick Anfuso, Martha Levin, and everyone at Free Press for believing in me and in our mission to present God's message of hope, love, and compassion to our world.

I also want to thank the best literary agents in the business, Jan Miller and Shannon Marven and the first-rate staff at Dupree Miller, for their friendship and loyalty and for thinking as big as we do.

When we stay in faith, God always brings the right people across our paths at the appropriate time and season. I want to thank

Joanna Hunt-Nunez for her dedication to this project and for the creativity and excellence she brought to it. I also wish to thank Michelle Adams for the many brainstorming sessions, and Ken Abraham who brought to this project the experience and expertise that only he could. And, of course, my thanks to Jason Madding for a great cover design.

I want to extend my warmest thanks to the staff of Lakewood Church for their dedication to our ministry. Together we are accomplishing great things for the Kingdom. In particular, I want to offer a loving thank-you to my executive assistant, Michelle Trevino, for keeping all of the balls in the air and consistently going above and beyond the call of duty.

I dearly appreciate and want to thank my Lakewood Church family, our faithful members who for more than twenty-one years have embraced me, encouraged me, and gone out of their way to show their love to me. They are my dear friends and a true reflection of God's love. And to the many people who view our television program and weekly podcasts, I say thank you for your heartfelt support and for sharing your stories and, in turn, your lives with me.

I am thankful that I have been surrounded

by a loving and supportive family all of my life. From the very beginning of my relationship with Joel, Daddy Osteen treated me like his very own daughter, and Dodie continues to show that same love to me today. Her life is an example of faith to me and many others. I have the best sisters- and brothers-in-law, and I am privileged to be close to Lisa and Kevin Comes and Paul and Jennifer Osteen on a daily basis. I am indebted for the devotion, love, and support that they and their families offer to me each day. And, I want to extend a special thank-you to my sisters-in-law and brothers-in-law, April and Gary Simons of High Point Church and Tamara and Jim Graf of Faith Family Church, whose faithful and godly lives inspire not only me, but thousands of others as well.

I was blessed to be born and raised in a faith-filled home. My father and mother not only loved me dearly and provided for all of my physical needs, but more important, they instilled in me the faith and values that I possess to this day. My mother, Georgine Iloff, is my best friend. She has always believed in me and expected the best from me. As a little girl, I wanted to be just like her. I still do. My father, Don Iloff, was my first knight in shining armor. He is the rock

— steady and secure. I am thankful for the foundation he provided and for always being there to pick me up when I fell. He never let me down. My brother, Don, is the best brother in the whole world. I have always admired his brilliance and wit, and I am blessed to have such a close and loving relationship with him, his beautiful wife, Jackelyn, and their daughters. I couldn't do what I do without his support and vision.

Finally, and most important, I want to thank my Lord and Savior, Jesus Christ. He is my everything.

CONTENTS

INTRODUCTION

I wrote this book in the hope that it will help you to achieve new levels in your life and to discover the treasures, gifts, and abilities within you that are just waiting to be uncovered. In the pages ahead, I want to share some foundational truths that will help you realize the depth of these valuable treasures you carry.

As co-pastor of Lakewood Church, I've had the incredible opportunity to meet so many women who share stories about their lives with me. We talk about their families, their careers, their good times and bad, and of course their relationship with God. Through many conversations I have found that although most of these women are doing good and important things in their lives, they often feel overwhelmed — emotionally, physically, and spiritually.

At a time when the pressures of the modern family are complicated by the pressures of the modern world, we often struggle to find a healthy balance between career, family, and relationships. But even in the midst of all the hustle and busyness, you can find fulfillment and achieve happiness — you can *Love Your Life!*

So what does it mean, to *Love Your Life?* When most people reach the twilight of their lives, they will tell you it's not about having a bigger house or a better job, or about the car they drove or the clothes they wore. They will tell you it was all about investing in themselves and their relationships with other people. How many times have we heard people say with regret, "If only I would have taken better care of myself . . . if only I would have spent more time with my family and the people I love."

That doesn't have to be you. Loving your life is being willing to make changes, to let go of old ways and unhealthy habits so that you can be the best you can be. It's about having the right perspective and understanding the value of who you are and what you have.

It's learning to love others and learning to love yourself so that you can get more out of your relationships. It's about recognizing the gifts that God has given you and making the most of those gifts.

Ultimately, loving your life is about discovering the greatness that's inside of you and the influence you have on the world around you. You will be amazed at the impact you will have when you tap into those treasures within.

No matter where you are today, you have the potential to have better relationships, to increase in confidence, to overcome obstacles, and to celebrate the life God has given you. Perhaps some unfair things have happened in your past, but those things don't define you and they don't determine your future. It's not what happens *to* you that matters most, it's what happens *in* you. You don't have to let your experiences draw confidence from you; instead you can draw confidence from your experiences. Be encouraged today because there is so much more in you that is waiting to be discovered. There are new options for your future, and opportunities to be recovered. Now is the time to leave the past behind and make room to embrace the destiny that lies ahead for you.

Let this book help you to see your life with a fresh new perspective: to see beyond where you are right now and to *Love Your Life* in ways you never thought possible!

1
Understanding Your Influence

What's in Your Memory Box?

A few years ago, my husband, Joel, and I were sitting in our living room looking through one of the many boxes of memorabilia my mother meticulously collected and organized over the years. We were doing some spring cleaning that day and stopped to enjoy the treasures we'd found in this one particular box. It was filled with so many reminders of who I was as a child — old photos, drawings, clips of my hair, and other childhood mementos. Joel and I were still laughing at a photo of me sitting at my mother's dressing table covered in her lipstick, when I came across a card that I gave to my mother and father when I was about seven years old. As I opened the faded, yellowing card, I read my own words of love and affection expressed toward my parents. "I love you, Mom and Dad. You are the greatest parents in the world." As I continued reading the card, my eyes were drawn to another part of the note written in red colored pencil, which simply read: "I feel like we are somebody important and I know that we are."

I stared at the phrase that I carefully printed so long ago and wondered why I would have written it. *What made me think of that? How could I possibly have felt so important? How could I be so bold at such a young age to think that my family and I mattered so much?* As I contemplated the words on the card, it was one of those moments that should have been so insignificant that I breezed right by it, but God opened my mind to an insight that has forever affected my way of thinking. That is, God has placed great value, significance, and importance on the inside of every one of us. That note I wrote as a child reminded me that I am important to God today, and because I am important to God, I am important to myself and to those around me.

What's in the memory box of your heart? How do you see yourself? Some days, you may wake up and not *feel* that important; in fact, some days, you may feel just the opposite. We all have days when it seems as though life is trying to knock us down and get us off course, and we lose sight of the great treasure inside us. But what matters most is not how you may *feel* or how you appear to others; what matters most is what you *believe* about your own value and significance.

We must remind ourselves every day that we are not here by accident; we are created in the image of God and our lives are full of purpose. Not only does our purpose involve our own accomplishments and destiny, but it also involves bringing good and adding value to the people around us.

Listen to what you are saying about yourself. What thoughts are you playing in your mind? It is extremely important to be aware of your internal dialogue and make sure it is working to your benefit. Wrong thoughts and wrong mind-sets distort your sense of value and worth and cause you to fall short of your full potential.

One of the best strategies of a great coach is to get his team thinking in the right direction. He builds up his players and helps them believe in themselves. When his team goes out on the field, it's not only about their *ability;* it is about their *attitude,* their *mind-set,* and their *internal dialogue.* They go out feeling like winners — as if they have what it takes to do a great job. In the same way, you should go out on the field of life feeling like a winner, having a champion's attitude, because of what you believe about yourself. Get in the habit of speaking positive, faith-filled words over your life, because a healthy self-image is one of the greatest assets you can have. It will not only cause you to rise higher, but it will inspire others around you to live at their best.

The way you live your life matters! Think about when you toss a stone into a pond and it sends ripples across the water — in a similar manner your life "ripples out" and has influence on those around you. You may not think you have that much impact, but whether you realize it or not, the way you live is setting an example. Your attitude, your confidence, how you carry yourself, and how you interact with others is influencing people in the most subtle ways. *Influence* is simply the power to produce an effect without an apparent exertion. In other words, just by living your life you are producing an effect. If we fail to understand our full value and live without focus or purpose, the example we set allows the people around us to rationalize living in the same way. That is why it's essential to hold on to this truth: You are important! The way you live your life matters! Pen those words on your heart and hold them in your memory box. When you recognize your importance and respect yourself, living each day with a champion's mentality, you are honoring God and reflecting onto others the value He placed in you.

YOU ARE THE SPICE OF LIFE

You are the spice of life, created to bring zest and flavor to the world around you just by being yourself! In our family, I tend to be the one who's always laughing about something and trying to find the humor in everyday life. One time I was making a joke about something that happened, and admittedly it was a little corny. My teenage son, Jonathan, just rolled his eyes and shook his head, with a big smile. (I could tell he wanted to laugh, though.) We all knew the joke was a bust, but Joel immediately piped up, "You know, Jonathan, if it weren't for your mother, it would be pretty boring around this house." I took that as a huge compliment, because no one wants to live in a boring house. Just by creating a light-hearted atmosphere, we can enjoy each other more and can be more productive when we work together. A good sense of humor and a positive outlook can add so much value to the world around us.

Your unique personality and characteristics are qualities people need; you *can* inspire others to greatness. Besides adding flavor and zest to the world around you, you can make people thirsty for a higher level of living and motivate them to fulfill their purpose. Just by living at your personal best, your example deposits strength into others and empowers them to rise to new levels.

I heard a story about a newly elected mayor of a town in Ohio. At the inaugural parade, as he and his wife rode down Main Street in the motorcade, waving to the crowds of people gathered along the route, they passed a man who was calling out to the mayor's wife. The mayor asked, "Who is that man?"

"That is my old boyfriend," his wife responded coyly.

The mayor nodded his head, and said, "Just think; if you would have married him, you wouldn't be the mayor's wife today."

She smiled and answered, "No, if I would have married him, *he would be the mayor today.*"

Now, that woman recognized her ability to influence! The question is: Do you recognize yours? We all have many different roles we carry out in life; we are parents, brothers, sisters, friends, employees, employers. Whatever role you are in today, you can help set the course of victory for yourself and those around you.

THE WAY YOU LIVE YOUR LIFE MATTERS

Not only do you make a difference in your personal relationships, but you have tremendous influence on the job. Whatever career you are in today people are counting on you. Whether you are serving at a restaurant or serving on the board of a corporation, you make a difference right where you are just by living with a heart of excellence. Isabelle works as a receptionist for a small oilfield supply company in Houston. She is perfect for her job. She's bright, personable, and among the most upbeat people you will ever know. Everyone around her office loves her. If a coworker has a personal problem, she knows she can talk to Isabelle and Isabelle will find the silver lining. If others have good news, Isabelle is the first one with whom they'll share it. She is known as an encourager in times of trouble, and a celebrator when things go well.

One day Isabelle[1] learned that her mother had been diagnosed with a serious illness, so she took a one-week leave of absence to be with her. During that week, various people in the office took turns covering for her. It was an inconvenience for everyone as they had to put aside their own duties for several hours at a time to take phone calls and greet visitors.

Unfortunately, Isabelle's mother took a turn for the worse and Isabelle was forced to take more time off. She used vacation time and sick time, but before long she ran out of paid days and had to arrange to take unpaid leave.

After about a month, the company's owner felt that the burden on the others in the office had become too great. Like his employees, he also valued having Isabelle around, but he decided that the drain on their energies was too much to bear and made a difficult decision. He instructed the human resources department to find her replacement.

Soon word got around the office that the company was looking to replace Isabelle. Instead of seeing the company owner's decision as a relief, something unexpected happened. Her beleaguered coworkers gathered together and went to see the owner. They told him that they didn't want her to be replaced and that they were willing to continue covering for her. One by one, they told him that they would stay late to finish their own duties or make any other adjustments if he would change his mind.

It took Isabelle's mother another few weeks to recover well enough for Isabelle to return to work. During that time, her coworkers faithfully kept to their word and not only covered for her, but did everything else necessary to keep the company on track.

It was over those last few weeks that the owner realized how important Isabelle was to the morale of the people in his office. In the many years since he had founded the company, he had never perceived as irreplaceable any of the dozens of receptionists who had worked there. In fact, he was so impressed by the dedication of his employees to Isabelle that he pitched in, to everyone's surprise, and covered the phones once himself.

The owner understood the value that a positive person can bring to a work environment. He realized the positive influence Isabelle had on the others. When Isabelle finally returned, the owner asked her into his office and informed her that he was going to pay her for the time she had been away. He even remarked to one of his managers that Isabelle was "just like a company benefit." Today, Isabelle is the highest paid receptionist the company has ever had.

Like Isabelle, you can make a difference in the quality of life for those around you. People need your love, support, and encouragement. Take your position seriously and use your influence well.

There's a story in the Old Testament about a young woman named Esther. She became an orphan as a young girl and her life held little hope for significance. She had no position or power; she was merely one of many young women in her city. But something was different about Esther: She believed in her God, and she believed in herself. At that time, King Xerxes was looking for a new queen, so Esther's cousin encouraged her to go to the palace with the other young women who were being presented to the king. Because Esther had favor with God, she found favor at the palace, and after a period of preparation, Esther was chosen to be the new queen. In her new position, Esther had tremendous influence and favor with the king. But it wasn't her social position that made her influential; it was her *heart position.* She understood who she was and that she was a person of destiny.

That truth was instilled in her many years earlier when Esther's cousin Mordecai deposited words of faith and hope into the memory box of Esther's heart. When she was just a little girl, he would tell her, "You've got what it takes. You were born to do great things. You can make a difference with your life." It was that voice of victory and those words of encouragement that helped Esther recognize her value and understand her potential. When she became queen, those words continued to help strengthen her and give her the courage to rise up and confront the challenges she faced. She understood that her life was not just about herself, but was about using what God gave her to impact others. Esther had those seeds of influence ingrained in her long before she had a title. I am sure she doubted herself at times, but she hung on to those words in her memory box, and what she believed about herself built faith in her to fulfill her purpose. Esther went on to save the entire nation of Israel from being destroyed.[2]

What if Esther hadn't recognized the influence her life could have? She might have shrunk back and settled for an ordinary existence and missed the opportunity to have an impact that changed the course of history for so many people.

Is your memory box filled with positive words of hope and encouragement? Or is it filled with doubts, insecurity, and low self-esteem? Perhaps no one ever took the time to encourage you, or some unfair things happened in your life. Maybe someone walked out of your life, but that does not change your value or significance. You are still important. Don't let what others have said or done stop you from living with purpose and enthusiasm. You can't hold on to past mistakes and allow them to keep you from what you were intended to be. It's time to get a new outlook on life. It's time to clear out those negative memories and start fresh. If you'll rise up today and see yourself as God's special treasure, selected by Him and for Him, then no one can keep you from your destiny! Nothing can disqualify you from your purpose. This is your season!

As Mordecai was for Esther, let me be a voice of victory in your life. Take these words and put them in your memory box: You are a person of destiny. You have an assignment and are full of gifts, talents, encouragement, and love. You have rich treasures inside you that people need. You have more in you than you realize, and you can accomplish more than you ever thought possible. No matter what happens in life, hold on to this truth, even if you don't always feel strong. Even during the times when life tries to push you down or convince you otherwise, don't allow those treasures within to get buried under your circumstances. You can rise above disappointments, negative words, and unfair situations as long as you don't lose sight of your value. Hold on to your sense of destiny.

I am reminding you today of what you already know because deep down in your spirit, you know you have what it takes. You are created in the image of God. He made you exactly the way He intended, and He equipped you with everything you need. You have the strength to stand strong in the midst of difficult situations, and the wisdom it takes to make good decisions. Dare to be bold and believe that you are a person of destiny because you can leave your mark on this generation. You may feel like your life looks ordinary today, but you too are writing the pages of history! Hold on to these words and allow them to drive you to your destiny.

So many people lose sight of their own destiny because they feel trapped in their circumstances. Too often, just because we can't understand something or we can't figure out how to accomplish our goal, we adopt the attitude, "It's impossible." However, today I want to challenge you to look beyond your limits and consider God.

I was talking recently with a woman who was in a situation that seemed hopeless but had come to ask for prayer. She had made some bad choices in her relationship with her daughter. They were in strife and not talking to each other. Now it looked like their relationship would never be restored and she would not be able to see her grandchildren and be a part of their lives. She was so distraught. I didn't really know what to pray, and it did look like an impossible situation. As I was praying, I heard myself say something that I don't think I've ever said before. I said, "God, it looks like her hands are tied. There's nothing else she can do." Then something just rose up out of my spirit, and I said, "God, even though her hands are tied, I know Your hands are not tied." When I said that, something leaped in my heart, and a light of hope shined in that woman's face. She immediately changed her focus, and she became willing to see past the impossible.

Are you facing a situation right now where you feel like your hands are tied? In your marriage? Your career? Your health? Are the negative voices constantly playing over and over, reminding you of how it's not going to work out, or how impossible things seem?

Maybe that's true, that your hands are tied today in the natural world, and it's okay to admit, "My hands are tied." But always know, God's hands are not tied. He can do whatever is necessary to bring you through.

Remember, even when it looks impossible, even when we don't see a way out, or even when we've made poor choices, God's hands are never tied. His power is unlimited. Nothing is too difficult for Him. Not only are His hands free to help you today, they are stretched out toward you. He can turn around any situation. With God, you can overcome any obstacle. He can open up the right doors and cause the right people to have favor on you. God can soften hard hearts. He can give you favor with the authorities. He can cause people to change their minds.

You may not see a way, but that doesn't mean there isn't a way. Our job isn't to try to figure it all out; our job is to trust and believe God, knowing that we are people of destiny, chosen and equipped for His purposes. As you stay in faith, know that God will choose you even when people overlook you. Like Esther, when we don't feel like we can do it, God will give us favor with the right people. His hands are not tied. No matter what's coming against you, face it in faith. Don't back down. What God has done for others, He can do for you.

In the Bible, long before David was King, he had plenty of chances to fall into the trap of believing he was insignificant and his life didn't matter. He was overlooked by his father, criticized by his brothers, and regarded by many as just a shepherd boy. When the prophet Samuel came to his house and asked to see all the brothers so he could choose a new king, David's father didn't even consider David a candidate and left him out in the field taking care of the sheep. It was only after Samuel didn't select any of the other seven brothers that David was called in and eventually chosen. Even then, David's brothers spent their time serving in King Saul's army, which was considered prestigious and a position of honor. David, being the youngest, was still relegated to the shepherd's fields. He was seen as an errand runner, having to often take his brothers, "the important ones," their lunch. He could have easily let that affect his self-image; he could have gone around feeling insecure, without a sense of his own value. But even though it seemed like life had overlooked him, David knew that he was *handpicked by God.* He chose to believe against the odds, and eventually David was promoted.[3]

You may feel that you too are the errand runner or that life has overlooked you. You've done your best, but maybe you haven't seen the results you had anticipated, or you've been through some disappointments and now you're tempted to think, *Oh, what's the use? I'll never get out of this situation. I'll never accomplish my dreams.* But don't believe those lies. You are *handpicked by God.* When you go through setbacks or when people leave you out, remember, God is working behind the scenes. You may not see how you can overcome your circumstances, but God has a plan and He can make a way. When you stay in faith, you can overcome any obstacle and accomplish everything God has planned for you.

LEARN TO APPLAUD YOURSELF

When we lose sight of our value, oftentimes we will turn to the approval of other people and look for validation from a parent, boss, or loved one. We all need encouragement, and we should receive it from the people around us, but we can't let that be our sole source of validation. We can't wait for the people around us to applaud us; sometimes we have to applaud ourselves! When life seems to be dragging you down, you have to be the one to encourage and believe in yourself.

I was at the gym the other day on the treadmill having a conversation with a woman next to me who had just been diagnosed with cancer and had asked me to pray for her. I said, "Yes, I will pray for you, but I have to tell you something first." I looked her straight in the eyes and said, "You know, you ought to be so proud of yourself. Look at you! You got up today and came to the gym. You could have pulled the covers over your head and stayed in bed, but you didn't. Instead, you are facing this with great hope and faith. I admire you, and you should applaud yourself."

When she was reminded of her strength and tenacity, her whole face lit up, she had a big smile on her face, and she held her shoulders back. She recognized the importance of affirming herself and giving herself the proper credit. If we are going to live in victory, our main encouragement has to come from the inside.

Don't be afraid to applaud yourself today. You may be going through some difficult situations, but you have strength to make it through. It's great when you have people in your life to hold you up, but what happens when those people are not around? That's when you have to learn to draw strength and encouragement from the inside. That's why it is so important to fill your memory box with all your victories, and all the times you made it through some difficult situation. Fill it with reminders of how God protected you, and how you overcame obstacles in the past. When you rehearse over and over all the good things you have accomplished and you dwell on God's goodness in your life, you will have the strength to applaud yourself today. You will have all the encouragement you need to rise up and accomplish what you want to accomplish. Believe in yourself and give yourself credit for a job well done.

My husband, Joel, is always so good at encouraging himself, and out of that inner strength he is able to encourage and add value to so many people all over the world. I remember one time we were doing a television interview with a well-known journalist in another state, and we had a pastor friend with us. Our friend has a strong gift of encouragement and he always knows how to make you feel like you are the greatest person in the world. He's always building up the people around him. After Joel's interview, as we all climbed into the car, Joel said, "That felt good. I felt like I did really well. I knew exactly what I wanted to say, and I don't think I could have done any better."

Joel wasn't bragging; he was just pleased that the interview had gone so well. But our friend was taken aback by Joel's strong self-affirmation. Later on, our friend told us that conversation literally changed his whole outlook on life. When he saw how positive Joel was toward himself, our friend realized that he needed to applaud himself more often. He was always so encouraging and complimentary to everyone else, but he discovered that he needed to encourage and compliment himself as well.

So often it's easy to see the good in other people, yet ignore the good qualities in ourselves. Not that we should be egotistical or boastful, but we need to see the good in ourselves and applaud even the little accomplishments in our lives. Did you complete a project you'd been putting off? Applaud yourself. Were you nice to a difficult person in your life? Applaud yourself. Are you overcoming an addiction? Applaud yourself! Don't wait for other people to validate you; validate yourself today. Life may not have turned out the way you planned, but you are still here, and you have value and purpose. Start looking at the positive and you will move forward.

Sometimes it's easy to feel overwhelmed with all the busyness of life. If we're not careful, we'll start criticizing ourselves, thinking of all the things we didn't do right that day. Maybe you didn't work out enough or didn't make dinner or . . . on and on the list goes. As soon as you recognize those self-defeating thoughts, you have to stop yourself and begin to acknowledge all the positive things in your day. Begin to look at what you've done right, instead of all the things you may be feeling. There is always something good you can find about yourself if you look for it.

Most people are their own worst critics, but instead, we should be our own best cheerleaders. It's easy to nitpick ourselves and go around being negative. But instead of bringing up the negative, start emphasizing the positive. Maybe you didn't work out enough, but you took the stairs instead of the elevator. Maybe you didn't take that friend out to lunch, but you did encourage the security guard on the way to work. You can find something that you did right. Maybe you've never actually said anything good about yourself. Start today by saying, "I'm a good parent. I'm a hard worker. I'm friendly and fun to be around. I'm kind and compassionate."

As you begin reminding yourself of all the things you do right, it will change your attitude. Before you know it, instead of being down on yourself, you'll start thinking, *I am pretty great!* Quit focusing on the wrong. Lighten up, because none of us is perfect. God is still working on us. If you're negative toward yourself, it not only sours your life but hinders your growth. You have to love yourself for who you are, because if you don't love yourself properly, you can't love others properly. That source of strength has to come from within. You can't expect other people to validate you all the time; you have to know that God validates you, and you have to learn to validate yourself.

Carol was a bright, talented, and lovely young woman who experienced the pain of a broken relationship many years ago. Over the years, she was healing and growing stronger; however, as a single woman, she found Valentine's Day to be the hardest day of the year. It reminded her of her deep loneliness and she would find herself in tears every year, longing to be loved. One year, she decided that she wasn't going to allow herself to fall into that cycle again. Carol decided that if there wasn't anyone to buy her roses, she would buy them herself.

The night before Valentine's Day she went to the store, and since she couldn't decide between pink and red roses, she bought a dozen of each. She carefully displayed them in a vase on her desk, and the next day the office was buzzing. "Who sent you those gorgeous flowers?" people asked. "Oh, someone very special," Carol replied with a smile. For the first time she truly saw herself as special, and the people around her did, too. That simple investment in herself filled a void that for many years had consumed her. She stopped looking outward and expecting others to meet that need for validation and started showing love to herself.

It's funny how something as simple as flowers can make you feel so esteemed at any age. I can remember being in the sixth grade and doing something similar myself. The school was selling single carnations for Valentine's Day that you could send to someone in your class. My friend and I wanted to make sure we received some, so we bought each other five or six of them and wrote different messages on each of the cards. And of course we had more than anyone else in the class! We just smiled, looking at our pile of carnations, feeling so pleased with ourselves. We were being silly girls, but honestly, sometimes you just have to buy yourself some flowers.

I have found that the way we treat ourselves sets the example for how others will treat us. If you are constantly down on yourself, you will draw people into your life who treat you the same way. On the other hand, when you invest in yourself and see yourself as valuable, the way God sees you, then others will recognize your worth, too.

PUT YOUR OXYGEN MASK ON FIRST

If you have ever flown in a commercial airplane, then you have heard the flight attendant's instructions, informing passengers about airplane exits, emergency lighting, flotation devices, and oxygen masks that fall from above your head in case the cabin loses pressure. Then the flight attendant will say something like this: "Place the oxygen mask over your nose and mouth before assisting children or those around you."

That truth plays out off the airplane as well. We have to take care of ourselves, if we are going to take care of anyone else properly. I heard someone say you have to "show up" for yourself before you can "show up" for others. Think about it — if you are empty, how will you have anything to give?

If you are constantly giving and never replenishing, you will be left drained.

We are God's creation and we have a responsibility to keep ourselves at our best. God never planned for us to live stressed out and overbooked. He created the world and all that was in it, and then He took the day off. When is the last time you took the day off or took some time to recharge your battery?

If you're like me, you make a to-do list every day: Run the kids to soccer, stop by the grocery store, finish a project at work. You rush here and there, taking care of all the things that matter most: family, jobs, friends, church . . . *oh, yeah,* did you forget to put *yourself* on the list? Do you need to move yourself up the list in priority? Most of us try to take care of everyone but ourselves, but I've found I am unable to give my best if I don't have my best to give.

I have a friend who has a great husband and three beautiful children. She is a good wife and mother, but she told me that she feels so guilty when she goes and gets her nails done. She feels like she has to rush when she is taking time to get her hair cut and colored. She said, "I sit in the chair at the salon tapping my feet nervously, just counting the minutes; I can't seem to relax.

I feel like I don't have time to take care of myself because there is so much that needs to be done."

It's funny because I am sure the only time she doesn't feel guilty is when she is doing things for her family. But the truth is, her family probably wants her to take time for herself so she can be her best for them. Don't fall into the trap of putting yourself last on the list or not even putting yourself on the list. That's not balance; it's not even healthy. You are important, so you must take care of yourself. That means you have to do things to relax — read, play golf, take a bubble bath — even if you have to schedule thirty minutes of "me time" into your daily planner. Sometimes just taking a walk in the park and looking at the birds or taking in some fresh air is enough to rejuvenate us. Maybe you need to kick back under a tree and enjoy an ice cream cone (fat free, of course!). Whatever it is that refreshes and refocuses you will be a good investment of your time.

Investing in yourself also means investing in your personal growth. Maybe you need to join a gym to get back into shape, or invest in some teaching CDs or leadership material. Sure, it can cost some money, but you're worth it, and the return will far outweigh the investment. You might be surprised at how a few small deposits in yourself can pay off in a big way. The important thing is that you take time for yourself and you enjoy it. If you had an expensive family heirloom, you would take care of it. You wouldn't mistreat it, let it get beat up or worn down, because it is valuable. You are valuable, too, so take care of yourself.

I read a story about a man who lived in a tiny apartment and who died in extreme poverty. At one point in his life, he had even been homeless, living on the streets. This man never had any successes to speak of, nor any noted victories. He lived and died as just another face in the crowd.

After the funeral, some family members went to his little run-down apartment to clear out his belongings. They found a painting hanging on the wall, so they decided to sell it at a garage sale. The woman who bought the picture took it to a local art gallery for an appraisal and was shocked to discover that the painting was extremely valuable. The piece of art that hung for so many years in a little run-down apartment had been painted by a famous artist who lived in the early 1800s. The woman decided to auction off that painting and ended up selling it for several million dollars!

Just think of how that poor man's life might have changed if he had known the value of what he possessed. He was a multimillionaire and didn't even know it! So many people today are living with priceless treasure inside, and they don't even know it. Sometimes we have to appraise what's on the inside of us to really understand what we have. Don't settle for living a mediocre existence. You are a masterpiece, created by the most famous Artist of all, but if you don't understand your value, you'll go on thinking, *I'm just average; I'm not that talented, I've made so many mistakes.* Don't allow those negative thoughts to play in your memory box. Instead, every morning when you get out of bed, remind yourself, "I am important. I am handpicked by God, and I am a person of extreme value and significance."

You are God's own masterpiece. That means you are not ordinary or average; you are a one-of-a-kind original! When God created you, He went to great lengths to make you exactly the way He wanted you. You're not meant to be like everyone else; God designed you the way you are for a purpose. Everything about you is unique and everything about you matters. See yourself as an original. When you understand your value — not only *who* you are, but also *whose* you are — then you will love yourself more, and you will love those people around you in a greater way. Realize today that because you belong to Him, you are extremely valuable. When you respect yourself you are honoring God.

After I found that card that I'd written to my parents so long ago, I started wondering if my children understood their influence in our family, our ministry, and the world around them. So one day I asked my eight-year-old daughter, "Alexandra, do you think you're important?"

"Yes," she said and smiled at me kind of funny.

I figured she wondered where all of this was coming from, so I told her about the note I'd written to my parents all those years ago and added, "See, when I was your age, I knew I was important, too."

She just sat there and grinned at me as if she were thinking, *Mommy, you're kind of weird, but I love you anyway.*

Joel and I want our children to know their worth. We want them to feel that they are an important part of everything we do. We want them to know that not only do they matter to us, they matter to God, and they matter to the world around them! You are never too young, and never too old to inspire the world around you.

When Alexandra was just five years old, she loved to sing and her daddy loved to hear her sing. One day Joel asked her if she would sing a special song at the end of our worship services on the road. Alexandra agreed, and I was so proud of her and impressed by her confidence. Here she was, just a little girl standing up in front of thousands of adults, and she didn't appear to be nervous at all. She stepped on stage and did what she loved, and she did a wonderful job. Now she regularly has a part in our touring events, and she always blesses the people when she sings. What amazes me most, however, are the letters we receive from parents and other children about how Alexandra's example motivates and inspires them. Children who were formerly afraid to participate in school or church programs receive inspiration from Alexandra's boldness, so now they are finding their own courage to step out and take part in things as well. Alexandra was simply being herself, and if a five-year-old can influence the people around her by using her gifts and abilities, all of us can!

You may never know all the lives you are

silently touching. You don't have to be on a stage or in front of a large crowd to make a difference; you are making a difference by living your life to the best of your ability. Have you ever been around that kind of person whose very presence inspires and motivates you to come up higher? When Jesus walked the earth, He had that sort of effect on people, and it wasn't because of His "superstar" quality or position and prestige. It was because He truly loved people and had compassion for them, depositing seeds of life and inspiration wherever He went. You too can have a positive influence in the lives of your family, your friends, and all those you encounter, even if it's for a passing moment.

YOUR LIFE PAINTS A PICTURE

Everything we do produces a seed and leaves something for future generations. The Bible says, "Let your light shine before men that they may see your good deeds."[4] Notice, people may not *hear* your words, but they are going to observe your life. I can tell my children all day long how they are supposed to act and what they are supposed to do, but the truth is they are going to do what they *see* me doing. When they grow up, they are going to model their lifestyles

47

and their relationships after what they have experienced. That is why it is so important to live as a positive example before our children and families. We paint a picture with our lifestyles, and our children put their own frame around it. Paint a picture that your children will be proud to frame! And remember, it's never too late to create vision and purpose in your home, and paint a picture that can be passed down in your family for generations to come. Recognize that through your example you are investing not only in your own children but in your children's children. When we recognize our importance, we are laying stepping-stones, not stumbling blocks, for future generations, and leaving a legacy of faith.

The Apostle Paul, when writing to Timothy, a young man who had great courage and confidence, told him, "Timothy, I can see the faith of your mother Eunice and your grandmother Lois in you."[5] Timothy's strong belief came through the influence of his mother and grandmother. Those women made an investment that had an impact in Timothy's life.

Maybe you don't have any children of your own, but perhaps there are other children in your life. Tell your nieces and nephews and your friends' children how important they are. Your words of faith will be a great deposit in their future. Invest in those around you, because you never know what can happen when you touch just one life.

In 1939, in a small East Texas town, a young man named Sam Martin would get to high school early each morning and write scriptures on the chalkboard. He was passionate about sharing his faith even though the other students thought he was a little odd, a little overboard, and they wouldn't have much to do with him. But one night a fellow classmate was walking home from a nightclub at two o'clock in the morning. He began to think about eternity and what he was going to do with his life. This young man went home and randomly opened the family Bible. The page he turned to had a picture of Jesus standing at a door knocking. The caption read, "If anyone will open the door, I will come in."

The teenager's heart was stirred. He recalled the scriptures he had seen Sam write on the blackboard. The next day the young man asked Sam about the picture and the scriptures he saw the night before. "Sam, why do you think I'm feeling this way?" he asked.

"That's God drawing you," Sam explained simply.

The next Sunday Sam took his new friend to church. It was that day that John Osteen, Joel's father, made a decision for Christ and his life of faith began.

Sam went on to become a pastor, but he never spoke to large crowds of people like my father-in-law grew up to do. Sam didn't make an impact around the world like John Osteen. But that didn't matter. If it wasn't for Sam Martin's positive influence, there might not have been a John Osteen or a Joel Osteen today. Fifty years later, Sam Martin wrote a book and called it *I Touched One, but He Touched Millions.* That should be the title for each of our lives.

Your life is significant. You are a part of God's eternal plan. You have a pivotal role to play in history. Don't ever underestimate your value. You may not be in the spotlight, but you will be rewarded for every good deed, for every person you encourage, for every act of kindness. When you touch one person, you are building a legacy of faith.

Loving your life starts here with the essentials: understanding you are important, and out of your importance, knowing you are called to add value to the world around you. No matter where you are in life today, you have potential to increase, to grow, to be strengthened, and to move forward. There is much more inside you that is waiting to be discovered.

In the famous movie *The Sound of Music,* there's a scene where Maria has gone back to the convent in hopes of escaping a difficult situation and discovering something new about the direction for her life. By way of encouragement, the Reverend Mother simply says, "You have to live the life you were born to live."

That's what I'm telling you today. Keep pressing forward into the life you were born to live. Keep climbing those mountains. There are new levels in your life and you need to look for them; there are treasures within you to discover, and there are gifts and abilities that are waiting to be uncovered. As you discover the valuable treasures in the depths of your heart, you will see yourself with a fresh new perspective; and you will *love your life* in ways you never thought possible.

ANCHOR THOUGHTS

I will fill my memory box with good things, recognizing my importance, living with a champion's mentality.

I will not hold on to past mistakes, nor allow them to keep me from who I was created to be.

I will not wait for others to applaud me. I will focus on my good qualities and I will applaud myself.

I realize I am handpicked by God. I will live with confidence, knowing that I am valuable and have something great to offer.

I recognize that everything I do produces a seed and lives on. I will be my best each day and plant seeds of blessing and favor for my children and future generations.

I believe God made me exactly the way He wanted, and He equipped me with everything I need to live an abundant, fulfilled life.

When it looks impossible and I don't see a way out, I will stay positive and hopeful, knowing that God's hands are never tied.

2
LIVING WITH CONFIDENCE

A few years ago, Joel and I along with our children would pile on the sofa after dinner to watch one of our favorite television programs, *Fear Factor.* We enjoyed viewing the contestants as they attempted outrageous stunts — from jumping off buildings, to sitting in a bed of reptiles, to eating nasty bugs. We'd sit and watch in anticipation wondering what the contestants would have to do next. And of course when it came to eating insects, Alexandra would bury her face in her daddy's chest while Jonathan would perk up and exclaim, "Cool!"

I'd choose a different word: "Gross!"

Each stunt tested the contestant's ability to confront and overcome his or her fear. If the person allowed fear to stop him, or even if fear slowed him down, the contestant would be off the show and the camera would follow him down the dreaded walk of shame. This continued until only one contestant remained. That contestant was of course declared the winner and received the prize money.

I noticed that most of the time, the contestant who won not only overcame her fear but approached each task differently from the others — with confidence. Her confidence not only allowed her to overcome her fear, but it allowed her to perform the tasks faster, more skillfully, or with whatever proficiency the task required. Many times we could tell who was going to win within the first twenty minutes of the show, just by that confidence factor. You could see it in the winner's eyes.

While that was only a television show, how often do we see a similar scenario play out in our own lives? We set out to complete a mission and we have our goal in mind, only to run straight into a wall of fear. Maybe you're about to apply for a promotion at work; then you find out someone that you perceive to be more qualified is also applying, so you shrink back. Or maybe there's something you've wanted to do for a long time, perhaps start a business or go back to school, but you're afraid you won't be good at it, so you stop.

It doesn't take a television show to know how effectively fear can block us from pursuing our dreams. Fear is the enemy of confidence. It can keep you from your God-given destiny.

The only way to break the power of fear and build confidence is to move forward. Confidence isn't built by playing it safe. It's not built when you simply stand still. It's built when you press past your fear. Throughout life, we all have opportunities either to shrink back and settle where it's comfortable or to take a step of faith and embrace the new things God has in store. You were never created to be stagnant. You were never created to take that walk of shame; you were created to win. Don't allow fear to hold you back. Keep stretching, keep growing, keep learning. Tap into everything God has put on the inside of you.

GOD IS CERTAIN OF YOUR ABILITIES

Most people are familiar with world-famous boxer Muhammad Ali, and his renowned trainer Angelo Dundee. What most people don't know is that just before every boxing match, Dundee would write a number on a small slip of paper and place it inside Ali's glove. That may sound like a strange thing to give a boxer right before a fight, but Dundee had a reason for what he did. The number that Dundee wrote on the slip of paper was the round in which he predicted Ali would knock out his opponent. Dundee was so confident in Ali's ability that he didn't just guess *whether or not* Ali would win, but *when* he would win — and Ali knew it.

I love that story because it shows the confidence Ali's trainer had in him, and it shows the positive effect it had on Muhammad Ali. I believe that confidence played a tremendous part in the champ's amazing success as one of the greatest boxers who ever lived. Dundee was certain of Muhammad Ali's ability to succeed, and the confidence that he instilled in his friend helped to give Ali a champion's mentality.

In the same way, God is certain of your ability to succeed. After all, He placed it there. Even when you're not certain of the outcome, God has confidence in you. Let that sink down into your heart today — the God who holds the universe in the palm of His hand has faith in you. When you really embrace that truth, it will cause you to have a champion's mentality.

Do you think Muhammad Ali was ever afraid? Do you think fear was a factor before he entered the ring to trade blows with the likes of Sonny Liston, Joe Frazier, or George Foreman? My guess would be yes. But I am certain that when he felt that little piece of paper in his glove, he knew without a doubt that the man who knew him best believed in him. That is when he pushed past his fear and marched toward his destiny. The little piece of paper that Angelo Dundee planted inside Ali's glove may have done more to make Ali the legend he is today than most people will ever know.

You may not be a professional boxer, but if you look deep inside yourself you will also find that something has been placed in you by the One who knows you best. God knew you even before you were born. He knows your abilities better than anyone else, and He believes in you. When He created you, He planted inside of you His seeds of greatness. Everything you need in order to be successful in your relationships, on your job, and in every area of your life is inside you.

Have you ever stopped to think about how a seed works? A seed is actually dormant until it is placed in the right conditions. You can have seeds for every kind of tree, plant, or flower tucked away in a drawer for years and nothing will happen. Those seeds are full of tremendous potential just waiting for the right environment. At any time, you can take those same seeds and plant them in the right soil, then give them the water and nutrients they need, and those seeds that were once dormant will begin to grow and produce.

The same is true for the seeds inside you. Those seeds may have been lying dormant, but you are still full of tremendous potential. It's time to change your internal environment so those seeds can grow and produce the harvest for which they were intended.

The fact is, if Muhammad Ali didn't know that little piece of paper was in his glove, it would have had no effect. Likewise, it is important that you recognize and understand what God has placed inside you — seeds of strength, joy, peace, and His vision for your life. Once you understand this, you will be able to push past your fears and uncertainties with confidence and move into your destiny.

When you think about it, the little note that Angelo Dundee placed in Muhammad Ali's glove was really just a piece of paper with a number on it. It did nothing until it became a part of Muhammad Ali's thinking. In much the same way, the seeds that God placed inside of you can lie dormant until they are planted in the soil of your mind. I encourage you today, open your mind and your heart and ask God to bring your seeds to fruition. When fear comes against you, His seeds will spring to life and give you the confidence you need to push past that fear and into your destiny.

This is what Joshua and Caleb did in the Old Testament. The children of Israel had just been led by Moses out of Egypt and were on the verge of entering the land that God had promised them. This land was already inhabited by others, so Moses sent twelve men — among them Joshua and Caleb — to scout it out and report back to him. The twelve men slipped quietly into the land and observed the people who lived there.

The inhabitants were huge people — giants — who were strong and powerful. Certainly, when the twelve Jewish spies saw the giants, those spies were awestruck. I can imagine that over the many days the twelve observed these giants, they saw things that caused fear to rise up in their hearts. Perhaps they watched the giants practicing their fighting skills or saw workers carrying huge boulders larger than those most humans could have carried. Apparently, whatever they saw struck fear in most of the spies. I cannot help but imagine that, like the others, Joshua and Caleb were impressed by what they saw. No doubt they too were tempted to fear the giants.

But Joshua and Caleb had a spirit different from that of their companions. They understood what was inside of them. While the others told Moses, "We are but grasshoppers compared to the giants," Joshua and Caleb declared, "We are well able to overcome. Let us go at once and possess the land."

Because Joshua and Caleb allowed God's seeds to take root, they were able to push past their fears and march into their destiny. They were the only two out of that whole group that ever made it into the Promised Land.[6]

Sometimes it is our own lack of experience that keeps us from trying something new. We want to do something fresh and exciting, but as we gaze into the unknown, we just can't take that first step. Perhaps you have an opportunity to start a new career, but you are afraid that you won't be able to succeed. Or your lack of experience as a homeowner has stopped you from buying your first home. While it may be true that you lack experience, let me assure you that God does not. He created the whole world, and when you rely on Him, He will give you the confidence you need to press past that fear.

God wants us to grow and move into our

destiny. When you follow His plan for your life, it is certain that you will sometimes find yourself in uncharted territory. But like Joshua and Caleb, when you understand who you are and that God is directing your steps, you can embrace your future with confidence, knowing that you are well able to do what God has placed in your heart. Take a step of faith today, and even if you feel fear, don't let it paralyze you.

I can remember how much fear I had to overcome when Joel and I took over as pastors of Lakewood Church. I didn't have much experience in public speaking and I dreaded getting up each Sunday and speaking in front of thousands of people. I would find myself uptight all week long. My mind was racing, full of anxiety and thoughts of doubt and defeat. It was as if there were a line of fear right in front of me that was trying to influence me to quit. One day I realized what was happening. That dread I felt was a symptom of fear that was trying to paralyze me. It was threatening to keep me from stepping into a new experience and growing to the next level.

Joel encouraged me repeatedly, "Victoria, we are in this together. If we are going to take this ministry to the next level, we both need to do our part."

Even though I recognized it was fear trying to stop me, that didn't make it any easier. The fear didn't go away just because I recognized it; I had to recognize something else: that God had planted seeds in me that enabled me to do what I needed to do. I could allow those seeds to spring forth and give me the confidence I needed, or I could allow them to remain dormant and surrender to the fear that was paralyzing me. I made the decision that I was not going to allow fear to hold me back.

The next time I stepped onto the platform, in my mind's eye I envisioned myself bigger than that fear. I kept telling myself that I am strong, talented, and able. I continued to plant those seeds in my mind, and as I did, I could feel my confidence growing. I saw myself moving forward, stepping over the line of fear. I envisioned God waiting right there for me with open arms, giving me strength and confidence.

From then on, every time I approached the platform, I visualized that scene until my fear was replaced with confidence. It was as if my seeds had developed into full-fledged oak trees. Now each time I step onto the platform to speak, I tell myself, "God chose me, and He has equipped me, and I am able to do what He says I can do."

These were my seeds. I encourage you to find yours. Don't allow fear to paralyze you or to keep you from achieving your goals.

Victory starts in your mind. When you know that God is for you and that He has a good plan for you, your seeds will germinate and spring forth. You will see yourself as He sees you, capable of overcoming the paralyzing fear that blocks your way.

I can imagine that when Moses died and Joshua took over as leader of the Israelites, he must have been a little intimidated. After all, Moses was the man who had led the Israelites out of captivity, parted the Red Sea, and drawn water from a rock. No pressure for Joshua, huh?

When it was time for Joshua to step into that leadership role, God spoke to him and said, "Move forward, I will be with you."[7] Joshua made the choice to step over the line of fear intended to paralyze him. Inadequate as he felt, he took action and moved forward to receive the blessings that awaited him. There are blessings that await you, too, when you make the choice to take a step of faith.

I have a plaque hanging on my back door reminding me of this very thing. In big black letters it says, "Move forward, I will be with you." Our whole family sees it when we come into our house and when we leave. Those words live with me. I think about those words whenever fear threatens to paralyze me. I pray that those same words touch your heart and inspire you to press past the fear that threatens to paralyze you.

I've heard it said that the road to success is paved with failures. George Herman "Babe" Ruth is one of the greatest baseball players of all time. He hit 714 home runs, and for almost four decades he held the major league lifetime home-run record. Legend has it that during the 1932 World Series he actually pointed toward a spot on the outfield wall and then proceeded to hit a home run directly over that spot. He was known as "The Babe," "The Bambino," and "The Sultan of Swat." In fact, Yankee Stadium itself is still known today as "The House That Ruth Built." He was a legend even during his own time.

One thing that many people don't know about Babe Ruth is that he once held the record for being struck out. That's right — three strikes, and the Great Bambino was walking back to the dugout. Which means you can add "Strikeout King" to his list of nicknames. In fact, Ruth struck out 1,330 times, more than any other player in his era.

Here is an interesting statistic: He held

the lifetime record for being struck out before he held the lifetime record for home runs. You would think that at some point in his career, perhaps the day he officially surpassed the previous record for being struck out, he would have been a bit embarrassed. I doubt anyone would have blamed him had he just decided to skip the next game. But he didn't.

Baseball players and fans love to heckle the opposing team's players, and I imagine he got a lot of grief from the other Yankees as well as the opposing team's fans.

You might think that once he became the Strikeout King, he would have started doing things a bit differently. Perhaps he would have changed his batting stance or decided not to swing so hard. But he didn't.

You see, even before Babe Ruth became the lifetime home-run leader, he saw himself as successful. He didn't allow his past mistakes and failures to affect his confidence. He never saw himself as a failure. Instead, he saw himself on a mission — to hit more home runs than anyone else. He was not going to allow the fear of failure to get in the way of his destiny. He knew those home runs were inside of him, just waiting to burst forth.

What do you do when you strike out in

life? Do you just give up and throw in the towel, or do you stand strong, knowing that you're one swing closer to that home run? Fear of failure robs so many people of their confidence and causes them to sit out the game, languishing in the dugout of life.

But, just like The Babe, you have to realize that the seeds of greatness are inside you, just waiting to burst forth. Don't let your past mistakes or failures steal your God-given destiny. Realize that you are also on a mission, and that no matter where you've tossed your bat, you can pick it up, get back in the game, and keep on swinging, because sooner or later you will knock that ball right out of the park!

One of my favorite stories is that of Rachel Smith. Long before Rachel Smith won the title of Miss USA in 2007, she was making a difference in the world around her. Bright and articulate, Rachel graduated from Belmont University magna cum laude and stepped out in the direction of her deepest passion — helping underprivileged children. She worked as a volunteer, helping young girls in Africa.

Later that year, Rachel represented her country in the 2007 Miss Universe pageant in Mexico City. It had already been a difficult week for Rachel as the Mexican crowd booed her repeatedly at the mere mention of the United States.

The night of the pageant, she gracefully walked out for the evening-gown competition, wearing a gorgeous dress and stunning high heels. Suddenly her feet slipped right out from under her on the highly polished stage floor and she dropped straight down on her backside — right in front of a live audience and millions of television viewers around the world. Rachel got back up, smiling brightly through her embarrassment, and finished her walk.

When it was her turn to answer a question during the final phase of the competition, the crowd started booing again. She chose a judge to ask her a question, and the judge asked, "If you could relive any moment in your life, what moment would you relive?"

How many times have we thought about our past mistakes and failures and said, "If only I could have the opportunity to relive *that* time in my life, I'd do it differently. I wouldn't make the same mistakes." Think about it: If you had the opportunity to change the most embarrassing moment of your life, wouldn't you? I know that if I had been Rachel and had just slipped and embarrassed myself in front of millions of people on global television, I might have responded to the question by saying "I'd like to relive my life about ten minutes ago in a different pair of heels!"

But Rachel didn't think that way. In fact she wasn't focusing on her past failures; she was focusing on her strengths. With a huge smile and all the confidence and dignity in the world, Rachel told the heckling crowd that the moment she would relive was when she was working with orphans in South Africa. What a great choice! Instead of reliving the moment when she was at her lowest, Rachel chose to relive the moment she was at her highest. The crowd continued to boo as she kept graciously smiling. "Buenos noches, México!" she said. And then she winked at the booing audience and gracefully walked back to her place in line.

Rachel didn't win the competition that night, but she won a victory that she will take with her the rest of her life. She overcame the negative, booing voices and walked away with an impressive title of fourth runner-up. The competition was over, but the story of Rachel's fall was all over the news and the Internet, and had over two million replays on YouTube.

We've all fallen. We've all heard voices trying to tear us down, but just like Rachel, we can't replay the falls. Fortunately most of us will never fail on worldwide television. Most of us will never see our most embarrassing moment on YouTube. But sadly, many of us will allow the fear of failure and embarrassment over our past mistakes to rob us of our confidence and our God-given destinies.

Don't make the mistake of replaying the negative images on the YouTube of your mind. Like Rachel, replay your victories. Replay your accomplishments. Replay the good things God has done in your life. Get right back up again and keep moving forward.

People boo for so many reasons. There may be critics at your job or in your family. People may be jealous or insecure, or they may simply misunderstand you. Maybe they aren't even booing you; maybe they are booing something you represent. Don't let the opinions of other people steal your confidence or cause you to shrink back.

If Michael Jordan had allowed people to rob him of his confidence, we would never have known the man who is perhaps the greatest professional basketball player of all time. When Michael Jordan was in high school, he had a coach who had no confidence in him. The coach saw very little talent in the young man, and as a result cut him from the high school basketball team. Michael failed, and he failed at an age when many kids would have just given up; but not Michael Jordan. He knew what was on the inside, and he did not allow that high school coach to rob him of his confidence. He worked harder, longer, and never gave up. He searched for, and finally found, the seeds of greatness that God had placed on the inside.

Remember, God did not create a failure when He created you. He did not breathe His life into a mistake. Remove anything that creates a picture of failure in your thoughts and choose to see yourself succeeding.

Instead of allowing your past mistakes to rob you of your confidence, focus, instead, on those times when you succeeded. When you do this, you will begin to recognize your seeds of greatness for what they are.

One of the great stories in the Bible is about a shepherd boy named David who defeated a giant named Goliath with nothing but a single stone and a simple slingshot. Everyone marveled at David's boldness and ability to take on such a warrior, but it wasn't by accident that David had the confidence to slay Goliath. He didn't just wake up one day and decide to take out that nine-foot-tall giant. He relied on the confidence that came from his past successes.

Long before David became king of Israel, he was a mere shepherd boy looking after his father's sheep. One day while David was tending the sheep, a hungry lion approached with every intention of dining on one of David's sheep. We know from the Bible that David had a strong and abiding faith in God. Though he was young and inexperienced and almost certainly feeling fear when he saw the lion, he placed his faith in God and stood up against the beast. The Bible tells us that he killed the lion.

On another day, while he was once again tending his father's sheep, a hungry bear approached, also intending to make a meal of David's sheep. With one dead lion under his belt, David once again put his faith in God and killed the bear. Surely his confidence was growing.

Finally, on one fateful day when he was tending his sheep, he was summoned to bring some food to his brothers who were soldiers. He arrived to find his brothers along with the army of Israel in a face-off with the army of the Philistines. There on the battlefield that separated the two armies was a nine-foot-tall Philistine warrior shouting obscenities at the army of Israel and challenging them to send a champion to fight him one on one. To David's dismay, there were no takers from among the Israelites.

When we read the account of this event in the Bible, there is only one thing missing from David — fear. In fact, David's response is filled with confidence: "Who is this uncircumcised Philistine who defies the God of Israel?" he asked. And then he volunteered to go alone and fight the giant warrior.

His brothers, along with the other soldiers, ridiculed him for what they perceived as mere bravado. But they did not know what David knew: God had placed the seeds of a warrior and a king inside him. His confidence became apparent when he proclaimed, "I have killed a lion and a bear. This Philistine is nothing to me." David possessed no fear because he was filled with the confidence of his past successes. I imagine that once you have fought and killed a roaring lion and a ferocious bear, a nine-foot-tall man just doesn't scare you.

God had prepared David for this day. David knew that if God was able to deliver him before, He would do it again. David did not see a nine-foot-tall man; he saw his victory over a lion and a bear. David drew confidence from his past experiences. By focusing on his past victories, he was able to recognize the seeds that God had placed inside of him, which caused them to spring forth and produce victory in his life.[8]

GAINING CONFIDENCE IS A PROCESS

David faced Goliath with confidence, but what if David had not faced down the lion and the bear? What if he had run when the lion approached or had just stood at a distance, paralyzed by his fear, as the bear slaughtered his father's sheep? Without those past successes, David's seeds would never have taken root and he would have undoubtedly reacted to Goliath the same way his brothers had — frozen in fear, trembling on the sidelines.

Gaining confidence is a process. You don't get it all at once; it happens only by taking one step at a time through your experiences. Your past experiences have prepared you for where you are right now, and your experiences today will prepare you for your future.

Any time you step out to do something for God or try to go beyond where you are, there will be challenges, obstacles, and discouragement. But don't let that stop you. Reaching new levels and gaining confidence isn't always easy — but it wasn't meant to be easy. If everything were easy all the time, you wouldn't stretch. You would never learn to recognize the seed of greatness that God has placed inside of you. Your seeds would lie dormant, and you wouldn't grow. Gaining confidence is a journey that is achieved one step at a time.

Stretching is good for your body, and it's good for your mind. It expands you and keeps you open for new growth. God wants to stretch you so He can increase you. He wants you to constantly be trying to do a little more than you are doing today, so you can tap into all that He has placed on the inside of you.

Every experience that causes you to stretch builds your confidence. God begins to work *in* you, and then you begin to work *with* Him. The more new situations you experience, the more you will stretch, and the more confidence you will have. Sometimes stretching is uncomfortable, but it prepares you for the challenges that line the road to your destiny.

Quite often God will use other people in our lives to stretch us. Since I was about nine years old, my mother has been in the fine-jewelry business. When I was about thirteen, my mother began requiring me to go to the jewelry store to work with her. I didn't like to go, but my mother wanted me to stretch and grow. She was so proud to have me with her, but to me it was pure torture.

Here I was, a young girl who was expected to sell expensive jewelry to adults. I was intimidated by the whole experience. I would rather have gone to the dentist than wait on customers! I didn't think I was qualified to sell fine jewelry. Doubt often filled my mind. There was so much to know about diamonds, rubies, and sapphires that I did not know. What if a customer asked me to design a ring or a necklace? I didn't know how to do that. I was certain that there were at least a hundred ways to embarrass myself. Fear was always there trying to paralyze me. Sometimes, I actually hid in the back of the store until all of the other salespeople were so busy with customers that I had no choice but to come out onto the sales floor.

What I didn't realize at first was that my mother understood my fears and insecurities as well as my gifts and talents. She knew that I had everything inside me to succeed, but she also knew that I would have to move forward, one step at a time, if that success was to be achieved.

She began by asking me to stand next to her while she helped customers. Then each day she would instruct me on the origins and attributes of one gemstone or another. Gradually she began teaching me how to design jewelry. As I matured in the business, she would ask my opinion and often take my advice. She would congratulate me on a successful sale and give me pointers when I failed. She would tell me how much the customers liked me and how they asked for me when I was not there.

Eventually I became quite knowledgeable in precious gems and metals, and I learned to love jewelry design. In time, I became skillful not only at selling jewelry but also at buying jewelry for the business as well.

God used my mother to help me to discover my inner strengths. By stretching me one step at a time He was allowing me to see that I could succeed even in unfamiliar territory. Through my mother, God was showing me how to replace my fear with confidence, setting me on a path of success. It was in that same jewelry store that many years later I met Joel. He came in for a watch battery one afternoon and I sold him a brand new watch. He loves to say that I've been taking his money ever since. If I had stayed in my comfort zone, I might have missed meeting the man of my dreams. (Looks like Mother knows best after all!)

If you will allow God to do so, He will stretch you, one step at a time. He will put people in your path, as He did for me, who recognize your talents and are willing to help you discover your inner strengths. And He will keep those people close to you as He moves you through the process of replacing your fears with confidence.

My experience at the jewelry store taught me that God had already planted the seeds of success inside me; and through my mother, He taught me how to bring them forth. When I look back now, I realize it was great experience because it forced me to press past my fears and learn to tap into the strength and confidence I didn't even know I had. Now when I find myself in uncharted territory and I need to gain strength from my past successes, I begin there.

I have come to realize that people are a lot alike; we have the same feelings, fears, and dreams.

A lot of things in life don't necessarily feel good, but they are necessary to stretch you. In fact, the experiences that seem the most difficult are often the ones that bring out the best qualities in us.

Are you going through a season of stretching today? Is your boss causing you to get out of your comfort zone? Instead of making excuses to stay where you are, shift your mind-set and say, "This is stretching me, and I can do this." No matter how uncomfortable you might feel, don't shrink back from those difficulties or challenges. Instead, stand strong, knowing that God is taking you to new levels in every area of your life.

As a little boy, my son, Jonathan, took piano and guitar lessons. Just as is true with any child, there were times when he didn't want to practice. Of course he'd rather be outside playing, but he was learning discipline by practicing and preparing for his first recital. After months of rehearsals, the day of the recital arrived. I was so excited and so proud of him. As we were about to leave, Jonathan came to me and said, "Mom, my stomach hurts and I don't feel well."

As his mother, I didn't want him to feel any pain and it would have been easy for me to let him stay home. I knew he wasn't really sick; he was nervous about playing in front of a crowd of people he did not know.

I knew Jonathan had practiced his piece and I knew that he was quite good at it. So in the same way that my mother had encouraged me to stretch myself so many years before, I encouraged him to overcome his nerves and stretch himself. I had him sit down at the piano and play the piece for me. As I expected, it was flawless. I asked him to play it again, and once again it was flawless. Then I asked him, "Can you play it a third time with no mistakes?"

He answered, "Yes."

I asked him, "Do you know why you can play it again perfectly?"

"No," he answered.

Then I placed my index finger gently on his chest and said, "Because God is in here helping you."

Miraculously, his tummy felt better. We went to the recital. He played the piece flaw-lessly, just like clockwork; the crowd of parents applauded, and both he and I were very proud of him.

Today, not only does my thirteen-year-old son speak in front of thousands of people as we travel across the country, but he plays guitar in a youth band at church and is about to join the adult band that performs at our Wednesday night services. Where will his music take him? Only God knows. But what I do know is that Jonathan has more confidence today because he stretched himself and pressed through those uncom-fortable feelings so long ago.

It's amazing what you'll discover if you start exploring what God has placed within you. I'm always astounded when I read an article about an eighty-year-old man who goes skydiving, or something equally daring, for his birthday. To us, it seems amazing, but that man didn't just wake up one morning and decide to jump out of a plane. You can be sure that he has been stretching himself and trying new things his whole life. I'm sure he prepared for that jump for many years, and saw himself do it hundreds of times in his mind.

What are you doing to stretch yourself? Don't just sit back and wait for something to happen. Take a step of faith; be a student of life. If you're a stay-at-home mom, it may be easy to think, *I don't count; nothing I can do would make a difference.* But the truth is, you have so much to offer this world. There's much more inside of you than you think.

There's a story about a woman who was newly divorced, almost penniless, afraid of public places, and trying to raise two teenage sons. After several tragedies in her life, she developed severe agoraphobia and was afraid to even leave her house. She searched her heart for ways to support herself and her two sons.

She loved to cook, and all she knew to do for income was to make sandwiches and other simple foods. With the help of her two sons, she found a few customers, but because she was so uncomfortable leaving the house, she had her two sons deliver the sandwiches. Her business quickly grew beyond the size of her kitchen, and she now faced a decision. Would she stand still and stop growing, or would she confront her fears and step outside her comfort zone? Though fear constantly nagged at her, she recognized that cooking was the seed that God had planted inside of her. As she sat in her house, she could imagine her business growing, and she began to see success. She made a decision to stretch herself — one step at a time. First she decided to confront the agoraphobia that imprisoned her. Reaching deep inside herself, she was able to take a job as a chef at a local hotel.

Her seeds began to grow, and once again she experienced tremendous success. She was learning step by step that the gifts inside of her were seeds of greatness. A few years later, she opened her own restaurant, The Lady and Sons, right in the heart of Savannah, Georgia. The restaurant's reputation quickly spread, and before long, the restaurant received national recognition.

Paula Dean's restaurant was such a success that she eventually landed her own TV show, published cookbooks, and even had a role on the silver screen. Today she is one of America's most beloved television chefs, and it all started when she realized that the power that dwelt inside of her was greater than the fear that held her back.

Oftentimes people stay where they are in life simply because of fear. But do you know that fear isn't reality? It's only a thought in your mind. It's just like in that classic movie *The Wizard of Oz*. When Dorothy arrived at the Emerald City, the great Wizard of Oz appeared to be all-powerful and mysterious, and he made everyone tremble. He seemed larger than life. But when Dorothy and her friends pulled back the curtain, the "wizard" was just an ordinary man, blowing smoke and pushing a lot of buttons.

One of the most important things you can do in your life is to learn to pull back the curtain of fear so you can see it for what it really is — *the enemy blowing a lot of smoke and pushing your buttons.*

Whenever you're tempted to doubt your ability to accomplish something, recognize that feeling as a symptom of fear — it's not reality. Pull back the curtain on fear and believe that God is working in you, and that

He will complete what He has started.

Do you need more confidence today? Start by declaring, "God is with me. He believes in me, and I can trust Him." It doesn't matter how many times you struck out in the past; that next swing could be your home run. God is still on your side, and He's sure of your outcome. He's not wondering if you will win; He knows it's just a matter of time. Recognize the greatness that God has planted on the inside of you and allow it to spring forth. You are stronger today than ever before. You have more wisdom. You have what it takes. You are fully equipped to defeat any giant in your life. Look back over your experiences and marvel at how far you've come. You are a champion, and your best days are right out in front of you!

ANCHOR THOUGHTS

I will keep stretching, growing, and learning and not allow fear to hold me back. I will tap into everything God has placed in me.

I will not dwell on my past disappointments and mistakes. I will focus on the good things God has done in my life, replaying my victories and remembering my accomplishments.

I will stay focused and determined, knowing that I'm gaining more confidence and growing stronger each day.

I recognize that God sees me as a champion. He's already destined me to win, and my greatest victories are still ahead.

I will not be discouraged by setbacks, failures, or delays. I know God is in control. He's working in my life and He will complete everything He started.

3

EMBRACING WHAT'S IMPORTANT

One day I was in the kitchen at Lakewood Church, making some hot tea. Several other people were taking a break, too, and the place was buzzing with activity. I had my tea in one hand and a spoon in the other, and I was just about to stir when suddenly I looked up to see my little five-year-old nephew, Christopher, pushing through the crowd and running straight for me. Now, although Christopher is less than half my size, he's as strong as a lion and as solid as steel. On top of that, he doesn't recognize his own strength. I knew I had to brace myself for what was about to happen. A split second later, Christopher plowed right into me, grabbed me around the legs, and started squeezing me as tightly as he could! With all the energy he could muster, Christopher was showing me his love, and with all the balance I could muster, I was trying not to spill my hot tea! As much as I wanted to embrace Christopher, my hands were full, so I couldn't. I had to let go of what was in my hands first. As soon as I placed my cup and spoon on the counter, I was able to wrap my arms around little Christopher and return his embrace. Not only was I able to enjoy Christopher's love, I was able to give love back to him. *There was an exchange that took place when I let go of what was in my hands.* How often do we go through life holding on to things that we think are important? Sometimes we can get so busy and have so much in our hands that we completely miss out on the new things right in front of us. We have to be willing to put something down in order to embrace something better.

Is there something you are holding on to today, something that you know you need to let go of to make room for what God is trying to do in your life? Is your schedule overloaded? Are you clinging to a relationship that you know is destructive? Are your thoughts consumed with a situation from your past? You might even be holding on to something good, but good things can also keep our hands too full to embrace God's very best. That day in the kitchen, I was simply holding a cup of tea. It was neither good nor bad, but it was keeping me from enjoying Christopher and allowing him to be a part of my day.

THE GOD OPTION

One thing is certain in life: change. People change, fashion changes, technology changes, seasons change — that's why it's important to stay flexible and be willing to change in order to embrace the new things God wants us to do in our lives. Some people struggle with change because they think it's difficult or because they feel comfortable where they are. But if we aren't careful, we can easily become complacent and coast through life never really growing or experiencing that which we are capable of enjoying. God wants us to look for new opportunities to enlarge our lives, expand our vision, and increase our influence. He wants us to broaden our thinking so we can broaden our lives.

So many people today live narrow, limited lives. They limit themselves and their options to only what they see, or what they knew growing up. If no one else in their family went to college, they think they can't either. They let other people define their limits, or they allow their resources or circumstances to define their limits. If that's you today, realize that you are not limited by your past, the economy, or what you have been told you can or can't do. No matter what options you may think you have right now, there is always an option you may not be able to see. There's always another way. I like to call it the *God option.*

Think about the first television sets that came out so many years ago. The picture was in black and white only, yet people thought television was amazing and were thrilled with it! When color television was first introduced, many people resisted it. They had grown comfortable with their black-and-white TVs, and viewing life in gray was good enough for them. Color television was an option they just couldn't see. You might be seeing your life in black and white today, but God sees your life in full color. He has so much more to add to your life if you will be open to new experiences and new ways of thinking. I encourage you today, be willing to look beyond where you are right now and be open to what *God* can do in your life. You may not see any other options now, but remember there's always the *God option.*

Many times in our life, Joel and I had to be open to what we couldn't see and didn't understand in order to make room for what was in our future. This was especially true when Joel's father passed away. At first we couldn't see how so many details could work out, and it seemed that our options were limited. Up to that point, Joel had invested more than seventeen years of his life working with his father behind the scenes in the television ministry. Not only did they work closely together, but they were great friends and Joel's entire career was tied to his father's ministry. His father was the one ministering out front, while Joel worked behind the senses, building and expanding his father's television ministry. That is what he was trained to do, and that's what he enjoyed doing. But when his father died suddenly, Joel had to be flexible and open to a new way of thinking about the direction of his life. He had to let go of any preconceived ideas he had about himself to make room for what God wanted to do next in his life. It wasn't easy, but Joel had to reposition his thinking and let go of the mind-set that he was just a behind-the-scenes person. Although it didn't look as if there were many good options, when Joel let go and allowed God to reshape his thinking, he was able to get a vision for the future. He embraced the change and believed that God was using it to take us to the next level.

God has placed in you everything you need to rise higher, too, but you must exercise your *God option.* Keep yourself open to change, keep the right perspective, and don't automatically assume the worst. Even though it was difficult, we realized that Joel's dad had run his race, and now he had passed the baton to us. This was the time to stand up, not sit down. Joel's determination to be open and to make room for whatever God wanted to do was the key step that launched us into the ministry we are in today.

Have you experienced a loss in your life? Do you need to reposition yourself today? Whether it was the loss of a loved one, or the loss of a job, or even the loss of a dream, God still has a good plan for your life. Stay open and be willing to change. God always gives you the grace to move forward. He is a progressive God, and He always wants us to rise higher; He wants us to let go of anything that would try to hold us captive. Don't get stuck thinking that there aren't any good options. There's always the *God option.* Remember, your life has seasons; there is a season to mourn a loss, but there is also a season to press on to the new things God wants to do. It's so important to reach a point where you are ready to let go of yesterday and embrace the future God has for you. When you hold on to the past or old mind-sets, you are actually falling into a trap that was designed to keep you from fulfilling your destiny.

Have you ever heard how hunters used to trap monkeys? The hunters would fill a large barrel with bananas and then cut a small hole in the side of it, just barely big enough for the monkey to get his hand and arm through. The monkey, completely unaware of the trap, would reach his arm into the barrel and grab one of those bananas. But when he tried to pull his arm out, he couldn't get his clenched fist and the banana back out of the hole. The monkey wanted that banana so badly that he wouldn't release it. Consequently, the hunters would easily capture the monkey. It's interesting that at any point prior to the capture, the monkey could have easily let go of the banana and pulled his hand out of the barrel, but he was so focused on what was in his hand that he didn't even realize he was in a trap!

Many people live like that today — with both hands clenched, so focused on trying to hold on to what they have that they don't realize it is robbing them of the freedom and victory God has in store. Don't let that be you! Choose to release anything that's keeping you from God's best in your life. Don't get trapped because you aren't willing to change or reposition yourself or your thinking.

Faith is a process. God leads us one step at a time. He will always put inside you whatever you need to move forward. If you need strength, it's inside you. If you need hope, it's inside you. If you need joy, determination, encouragement, God has placed them within you. So tap into your God-given resources by faith, because He will never ask you to do something that He hasn't already prepared you to do. Be open-handed and open-minded to what God is doing in your life today.

In the Bible, God told Abraham to leave his homeland and go to a new place. It didn't make a lot of sense to Abraham because he was comfortable where he was. He had family and friends and he was familiar with the surroundings. He could have easily held on to what he had and said, "God, I like this place. I don't want to go. I like what I have in my hand."

But Abraham believed that if he let go of what was in his hand, God would give him something even better. Abraham stayed open to change. He and his family, along with his nephew Lot and Lot's entire family, packed up their belongings and their herds and headed out into the unknown. As time went on, they had increased so much that the land couldn't support both families and all the livestock, so Lot and Abraham agreed to part ways. Abraham gave Lot the opportunity to choose the land he wanted. He said to Lot, "Which direction do you want to go? You choose first, and I'll take whatever is left." Lot looked out as far as he could see in both directions and chose the best part of the land, the plain of Jordan. The Scripture describes it as a well-watered garden, so beautiful and lush. I imagine it may have looked like Hawaii, even though it was in the Middle East. When Abraham saw what was in the other direction, it didn't look like Hawaii; it looked more like the desert. It didn't look very appealing — there were few trees and little grass. It would have been easy for Abraham to think, *Man, I got the short end of this deal. God, where is the favor You showed me in the past? I'm the one who had the assignment. Why is this happening? If only I had chosen first!*

Have you ever felt that way? Have you found yourself thinking, *God, I expected one thing and I got something else?* I know I have. Sometimes the very thing we think is working against us is really going to work out for us. However, it's up to us to release our old way of thinking and embrace the change God has in store for us. That's when we have to rely on our faith to help us stretch and grow. God always wants us to move forward so we can tap into our full potential. If you have been going through some changes that you don't understand, or if it looks like you don't have the favor you once saw in a certain area, God could be stirring you out of the old so He can bring you into something new. It's not always comfortable, and it may not always be the easiest way. Sometimes it looks like we missed out, but if we will embrace the new and let go of the *if onlys,* then God can open the right doors and get us where we need to be. It's easy to overanalyze a situation or look to place the blame somewhere. It's easy to slip into thinking, "*If only* I had gone to college," "*If only* I had married that person," "*If only* I would have qualified for that new home." However, you must get past the *if onlys,* because you can't stay where you've never been! You have to look forward to where God is taking you. He has the right places, the right people, the right opportunities lined up for your future. It may look as though you missed the good, but remember,

God always has something better in store.

This is something Abraham believed about God. Abraham did not complain or criticize Lot for taking what was clearly the best land. He did not question God or gripe about getting the short end of the deal. I like to think that he looked out over the barren land that was soon to be his home and thought, *It's going to be exciting to see how God turns this around.* I am amazed at how Abraham let go of something good in anticipation of something better. And of course God fulfilled His promise to Abraham.[9]

Years ago when Joel and I first got married, we set out to buy a home. We found one that looked like it was perfect for us. It was located in a neighborhood filled with other young families, it was on a beautiful lot, and it even had a swimming pool — something that I've always wanted. We made the best offer we could on the property, and prayed and believed that the owners would accept it. Day after day went by, but we didn't hear anything. We kept speaking words of faith, declaring, "This is our house." No one was living in it at the time, so we would go out in the evening and look at it, study it, and dream about it. One time I even marched around it — like the children of Israel marched around the walls of

Jericho — believing God was going to give us that house. I was determined. I could see it and I could believe it! I thought, *That is my house!* But unfortunately the home-owners didn't take our offer. We didn't get that house. The door totally closed. I couldn't believe it. I was so disappointed. I thought for sure that was the house we were supposed to have. I found myself tempted to say *if only* we had offered more. *If only* we had prayed harder. *If only* we had acted sooner . . . and on and on. But instead of mourning over what didn't work out, instead of holding on to what was in my hand, my desires, I made a choice to let it all go and believe that God had something better in store.

If we are going to experience the best God has for us, we have to open our minds and be willing to change, and be willing to look for those *God options.* We have to remind ourselves that God always has our best interests at heart.

Right after we heard the news about the house, I went out and began looking at other houses and came across something that caught my attention. It was an old run-down house on a beautiful piece of property in a valuable neighborhood. The house was actually abandoned. It had a few broken windows, no landscaping, and even a scare-crow in the kitchen to keep out animals! It didn't look like much, but down deep I believed it was right for us — not because of what I saw, but because of what I believed God had in store for us. I knew if I would be open to see beyond the old house and look for the *God option,* I would get to where I needed to be. My heart was open to whatever God had in store for us. So we put a bid on that house, and just a few days later, we got word they accepted our offer.

The truth is, I wasn't as excited about this house as I was about the other one. This house didn't have a swimming pool; instead, it had crooked floors. The foundation was cracked and some of the interior doors wouldn't even close. I had to put blocks under my couch just to keep it from leaning forward. There was a long hallway going back to the bedroom, and I remember thinking, *I'm going to walk down the hall on one side and walk back on the other side just to make sure my legs don't grow unevenly because of those crooked floors!* Friends and family members used to make jokes about those crooked floors, but I grew to love that house. Even though it wasn't exactly what I wanted, I knew God gave me that house, so I wasn't going to look back and focus on the house I didn't get. I embraced what I had and made the best of it. And that's what we have to do in every area of life. We can't stay focused on where we thought we should have been, or what we thought we should have had. We have to let go of the old and accept where God has us today.

Sometimes the very things we fight against, the very things we think are trying to pull us down, are actually part of God's plan to launch us into a new season. Sometimes God stirs us out of comfortable situations and puts us in situations to stretch us and cause us to use our faith. We may not like it, and it may not always be comfortable, but God loves us too much to just leave us alone! We have to stay open to change. Don't approach change from a negative point of view or automatically assume it's going to be bad. You may not like the change, but God would not allow it if He didn't have a purpose for it. If you'll learn not only to accept change but to embrace it, God promises He will do a new thing in your life, and His "new" is always much better than the old! The key is to look for the potential and open your mind to the positive. That house didn't appear to be the perfect house, but it was the right place for that season of our life. We lived in that house for three years and God blessed us beyond our wildest dreams. We ended up dividing our lot and selling *half* of it for the same price we originally paid for the entire piece of property! We were able to build a new home for less than what we would have paid for the other house.

God used that crooked-floored house in our life in a powerful way. He brought us through a journey of faith. That's where we grew. That's where we learned to trust Him and believe that He always knows what's best. Today I'm not living in a house with crooked floors. I'm living in a house more beautiful than I ever dreamed we would own. I can see now that God was taking me on a journey of faith. Even though it looked like we were going backwards, it actually helped us move forward to where God wanted us to be. I'm convinced that if I would have been unhappy over what didn't work out, and discontented with where I was living, my attitude would have kept me from God's best. When I look back, I realize it wasn't about the house, but more about what God was doing in our lives — teaching us, training us, testing us, seeing if we would stay faithful and trust Him even when we weren't getting our way. I believe that if I would have gotten the other house, we wouldn't be where we are today. Our experience with that house gave us courage to trust God, to walk in faith, and years later, to take a basketball arena and turn it into a magnificent house of worship!

If you're thinking, *Life would have been different if only I had this or if only that had happened,* let it go. Let go of the *if onlys.* Don't get caught in that trap. Know that God is in complete control and He is guiding every one of your steps. Learn to trust Him. Even if life may not make a lot of sense right now, God has a plan. If you'll let go of those things that didn't work out and choose to stay in faith, then God will take you to where He wants you to be.

Remember Lot and Abraham? It's interesting that the name "Lot" actually means *veil.* When Abraham separated himself from Lot, it was as if the *veil* was lifted from his eyes and he was able to see things in a new way. God told Abraham to lift up his eyes and see beyond where he was. God told him to look beyond what he could see — that dry, desolate land — and look toward what God was doing in him. Today God is saying something similar to you: If you'll lift up your eyes and look out with a fresh vision and a fresh attitude, letting go of the old, then the veil will be lifted and you will see the new things God wants to show you.

God is all about bringing change for the better. When Jesus walked through the streets, He asked people, "What do you want Me to do for you?" I believe He's asking you that right now. What do you want Him to do for you? Do you need His help with your marriage? Is it your finances? Is it your health? Don't have an *if only* mentality. God always has another option. When you trust Him, when you stay in faith, He *will* make a way even when there seems to be no way. He will fill your life with blessings and treasures beyond your wildest dreams.

MAKING ROOM IN YOUR RELATIONSHIPS

My friend Shannon grew up with a heart for God, but as a young woman in her mid-twenties, her life became focused on other things. Her hands were full. Her career as a journalist was taking off beyond her wildest dreams. It appeared from the outside that she had a storybook life — complete with her Prince Charming. On the inside, however, their relationship was tumultuous, but it was one with which she had grown comfortable. Shannon believed that it was a good relationship and that she could change him, so she convinced herself to stay with the "prince."

Regardless of how comfortable the relationship had become, she still had restlessness in her heart. She knew they were not right for each other. One day Shannon received a job opportunity in another state. As she pondered her future, she realized it was a big change and the most difficult decision she would ever make. She would have to leave the comfort of her home, her job, and her longtime boyfriend. For the first time in many years, she prayed. Ultimately, she decided to make the bold move and step decisively into the unknown. As hard as it was, she left everything that was familiar to her.

Shortly after her move, she was making dinner in her new apartment when an overwhelming sense of loneliness and fear engulfed her. She began second-guessing her decision, wondering if she had made a big mistake. As she sat there with tears in her eyes, God dropped two words into her heart: "trust" and "obey." She realized at that moment it was time to rise up, let go of the hurt and pain, and move forward into the future. Her first decision was to start attending church again. She made room for God in her life and He began to heal and restore her. She experienced a great peace and comfort and was able to embrace the changes He revealed to her, knowing that God was present in her life again. As she began her new life, God opened doors for her to meet new friends, and eventually she met and married a wonderful man who truly surpassed her every expectation!

Shannon's restlessness was a result of the fact that God was trying to move her out of something that was not good for her, into something new, positive, and healthy. Her ability to recognize that something was wrong in her life, along with her willingness to trust God, gave her the courage to move forward. As she began to look out with a fresh vision and a fresh attitude, she was able to perceive the new things God had in store for her.

Today if you are in a relationship that is not right for you, don't wrestle with your feelings or make excuses for what's going on. I am not talking about a marriage relationship; I am talking about any relationship outside of marriage that you know is dragging you down and causing you to fall short of what you were intended to be. Are there influences in your life that you know are not right? Are you spending too much time with friends who are putting your destiny at jeopardy? Is there a commitment you are about to make in a relationship you're unsure of? If you are seeing red flags but you're afraid to let go because you don't want to be alone, remember, God will never leave you alone; you are too important to Him.

When one door closes God will open a bigger and better door for you. He may be trying to stir you out of a situation that is not good for you. Even if you are thinking of a friend who walked out of your life, realize that may be God helping you. He may have closed that door so you couldn't go back, preventing you from going in the wrong direction. God has such a great desire for you to reach your full potential. Be willing to recognize if there is something wrong in your life and have the courage to move forward, with a new perspective; be open for something bigger and better. Trust Him today; He wants you to have strong, healthy relationships so you can live your life happy, healthy, and whole.

I heard a story about a little girl who was carefully saving her money from her allowance so she could go to the toy store. She didn't have much, only a few dollars, but one day she asked her daddy to take her to the store so she could buy something special. She was overwhelmed by endless aisles of shelves, filled with games, dolls, and trinkets. Finally, a particular item caught her eye, and she knew it was exactly what she wanted — a lovely strand of white plastic pearls. She made her purchase and immediately went home to show off her treasure. She was so proud of that necklace; after all, she picked it out all by herself. She wore it every day for several weeks. Her father saw this as an opportunity to teach his daughter about trust. One day he asked her, "Honey, will you give me your pearls?"

"No, Daddy. I love my pearls!" she replied. "I can't give you my pearls!"

Her father didn't mention the pearl necklace for several days, and then he asked again, "Sweetie, do you trust me?"

"Yes, Daddy."

"Will you give me your pearls?"

And again she answered, "No, Daddy, I can't give you my pearls!"

Several more days passed, when the father went a third time to his daughter. "Do you trust me? Will you give me your pearls?"

Finally, with tears welling in her eyes, she reluctantly took off her beloved plastic pearls and handed them to her father. "Here, Daddy. You can have my pearls."

Immediately, the father pulled from his pocket a small blue box and handed it to his daughter. Her eyes grew wide with excitement as she opened the box to find the most gorgeous strand of genuine pearls. As he fastened the pearls around her neck, the father said, "I have had these special pearls for you all along; all you had to do was trust me."

Is there something you are holding on to today that is keeping you from God's best? If you'll let go of what's in your hand, an exchange will take place. God will let go of what's in His hand for you — peace, strength, wisdom, favor, and more! He'll give you exactly what you need. You may not see how it can happen. You may feel like you're out of options, but remember there's always the *God option.* And even if you don't get what you thought you should have — maybe you got crooked floors like I did — keep a good attitude. God is still in control. He's taking you on a journey through the process of faith. Be open to seeing things from a new perspective. Get a new vision for your life. It may not happen overnight, but it will happen. So open your hand and receive the beautiful strand of pearls God has for you today. Don't settle for plastic when all you have to do is trust Him!

ANCHOR THOUGHTS

I will stay flexible and willing to change in order to embrace the new things God has in store.

I will look beyond where I am right now, seeing new possibilities, being open to new ideas, and expecting great things in my future.

I will not live my life in regret. I make a decision today to release the *if onlys* and anything that is keeping me from God's best.

I recognize that even though challenges and difficulties seem like they're working against me, if I stay in faith, they will ultimately work for me.

4
KEEPING THE RIGHT PERSPECTIVE

One evening several years ago, I was sitting in my living room watching television when a commercial came on that really grabbed my attention. It was a simple advertisement that showed a lovely young woman strolling down a sunny street wearing a flowing dress, swinging her purse by her side, and all the while singing, "I've got a new attitude!" She was clearly enjoying her life and appeared as if she didn't have a worry in the world. It made me wonder where she found that fresh new outlook. She wasn't being naive about life, but rather she looked as if she were reveling in a recent victory and consciously making the most out of every moment of the day. Yes, it looked as if she had that new attitude because she *chose* it.

What's your outlook on life today? Do you wake up every morning ready to embrace the day? So many people allow their circumstances to dictate their attitudes; they don't realize their attitude is a choice. Scripture encourages us to constantly put on a fresh new mental attitude. When we wake up in the morning, we should choose to focus on good things; we should choose to be grateful; we should choose to be excited about the day.

It is all too easy to let our responsibilities and the pressures of life cause us to drift toward the negative. But negative thinking bogs us down and causes us to lose our joy and enthusiasm. Before long, we stop appreciating our friends and family; we start believing our boss has something against us. And we begin to wonder if the entire world has something against us. Negative thinking makes the small stuff seem so much bigger, until we are living in constant worry and frustration. If that's how you feel, take heart — your life can be different! You can take off that garment of heaviness and put on a garment of thanksgiving. That means by an act of your will, you can have a new outlook on life.

Remember, we all face difficulties. We all have obstacles that seem impossible to overcome. The difference between those who are able to rise above their adversities and those who get stuck in them is their *attitude.* A key to enjoying your life is finding something to be thankful for every day. Make a list. Write down all the good things in your life. Review it each morning before you leave the house. This will help you focus on the treasures that fill your life, and it will give you a positive perspective and a grateful heart. We all have things for which to be grateful, but sometimes our perspective can become so distorted that we fail to recognize those good things.

I have a friend who tends to lean toward a negative perspective. Whenever I call her to check in, she'll say something like, "I've had the worst week. Both my kids were sick, and I was late for work because the doctor's office didn't open until nine. I've had to stay late at the office, and now the house is a disaster. My husband still doesn't seem to know how to operate the washing machine, and the dust bunnies are battling it out with the Legos to take over the den."

Now, this friend really did have a rough week, but I've been hearing about her husband's shortcomings for the past eight years. He's actually a great guy; he takes the kids places on Saturday mornings so she can sleep in; he works hard and is supportive of her career. He has many marvelous qualities. Yet my friend chooses to focus on the negative, despite the fact that her life is rich in so many ways.

It's easy to have a distorted perspective — overlooking all the good things and magnifying the things that are wrong. No matter what season of life you are in, you must deal with the temptation to focus on the negative. Make no mistake, we all choose where to place our focus. Those people with the best perspective on life choose to be happy and content with what God has given them.

In the book of Genesis, Eve was a woman who truly had it all. She was living in the most gorgeous and lush garden ever, with the perfect man — literally! She enjoyed magnificent streams, rivers, and waterfalls, all surrounded by the most fragrant flowers, along with the freshest fruits and veggies imaginable. Just think: no weight problems or dirty laundry; she truly was living in paradise! Until one day when she began focusing her attention on the one negative in her garden — the single fruit tree from which God had warned her not to eat. The more she looked at the forbidden fruit, the larger it became in her mind. She allowed the one negative in the garden to distort her perception of the entire garden. She no longer valued the treasures within her paradise. Instead, she magnified that one forbidden thing until it was so large in her mind's eye that she could see nothing else.[10]

When you magnify something, it doesn't actually change the size of the object, it simply changes your perspective of the object. When you hold a quarter in your hand and stretch your arm out in front of you, the quarter seems small compared to your surroundings. But when you pull the quarter in nearer to your eye, it appears much larger. In fact, when you hold it close enough, you aren't able to see anything else. So often in life, our difficulties and challenges seem so much larger than they actually are, simply because we are holding them closer to us than necessary. But when we have the right perspective, those same difficulties become much more manageable.

To keep the right perspective, we have to magnify the right things in our lives. When I come up against challenges, I remind myself of all the great things God has done for me. I begin to thank Him for allowing me to know Him; I thank Him for my family, my children, and my husband. I recall past trials in which God made a way for me and brought me through tough times. I am always amazed how my perspective changes when I have a grateful heart and choose to count my blessings.

When we choose the negative, it's like

swimming against the current; it makes everything a struggle. An improper perspective will drain your energy and vitality; it will take the fun and joy right out of your life. Your life was meant to be enjoyed; you weren't created to constantly struggle and be perpetually discouraged.

As a first step toward a positive perspective, it's good to take inventory of your thought life. What are you thinking about? How are you approaching each day? Identify any self-defeating can't-do-it thoughts and decide not to dwell on them. You will be pleasantly surprised with the change in your perspective. Instead of dreading things and complaining about the situation, face each day with faith and enthusiasm.

When Joel and I first began traveling to various parts of the country with the ministry, it seemed that every time I turned around, I was packing or unpacking for a family of four, and it was getting to be quite stressful. I would get so concerned about having everything we needed that I would check and double-check and wake up in the middle of the night before we were to leave and check again. One day it dawned on me that I was wasting a lot of energy struggling with something that really wasn't all that important in the grand scheme of life. In reality, the whole trip wouldn't be ruined if I forgot something such as Jonathan's socks or Alexandra's toothbrush or my hair spray! Packing really wasn't a big deal at all, but I had allowed it to become a big deal in my mind.

I got to the point that I could feel myself grumbling and complaining about going on the road so much. I even took it a step further and thought, *Why do I need to go? Joel doesn't need me to help him. The audience won't really miss us if Jonathan, Alexandra, and I stay at home this weekend.* Self-defeating thoughts played over and over in my mind every time a trip came up. I would try to talk myself out of going. And I am sure at some point Joel could feel my tension. I allowed that wrong thinking to steal my joy, and it almost caused me to miss my God-given destiny.

Thankfully, when I realized how out of character my thinking had become in this area, I was able to take a step back and see it for what it was: I had allowed my worries and concerns to discourage me and distort my perspective. I decided right then and there that I wasn't going to be stressed out about packing for trips anymore. I said to myself, "I'm sure if I forget something we really need, we can buy it when we get there." I decided to let myself off the hook. That simple minor adjustment released me from an enormous load of pressure. Now when I find myself getting stressed out and tired from all the packing and traveling, I don't allow my mind to think self-defeating thoughts that will move me in the wrong direction. I switch gears and begin to move forward. I remind myself that this is an opportunity God has given us. He could have given it to many other wonderful people, but He chose to give it to us. That helps me put on a fresh new attitude and allows me to enjoy my future experiences.

I've heard it said, "Your attitude determines your altitude," and I believe that is true. Our attitude affects our progress. The better your attitude, the higher you will rise. If you are going through stressful times today, keep an attitude of faith and victory. As you remind yourself of all the great opportunities you have, it will make those tough times seem much easier, and you will rise to new levels.

ARE YOU LOOKING AT THE BIG PICTURE?

The other day I was having lunch with some friends, one of whom had recently returned from a luxurious cruise with her entire family. They had saved their money and had meticulously planned every detail of their trip months in advance. The trip had been especially meaningful because on this vacation, my friend was able to visit with some of her extended family that she had not seen in more than a year. She was all smiles as she pulled her newly developed photos out of her purse. She said to another friend and me, "Would you like to see the pictures I just got back from my family vacation? I haven't even had a chance to look at them yet myself."

We were happy to share in her excitement as we flipped through the photos, filled with images of the fabulous cruise ship, beautiful sandy beaches, charming island shops, and lots of happy faces. But before long, we noticed an uncomfortable expression on our friend's face. She began to complain about her appearance in the pictures. "Oh, I didn't know I looked like that! This picture is awful!"

She had something negative to say about herself in every picture. A few moments earlier, she had been so excited, but then she zeroed in on what she saw as her flaws and shortcomings. She completely missed the beauty of the moment. It was as if she couldn't see the big picture anymore. Instead of enjoying the memory of the marvelous trip with her family, she began to focus on her imperfections — little things that only she could see.

We all have times when it's hard to see the big picture and we single out what we think is wrong about our lives. But we have to recognize that we will never get that time back; we must enjoy every day. Don't long for the good old days. These *are* the good old days, so make them count!

Years ago, we were having a big Easter service at Lakewood. Our family — in-laws, cousins, aunts, and uncles — was all dressed up, everybody looking especially sharp in their Easter Sunday outfits. We planned to take pictures with everyone after the service. There was a lot going on when church dismissed, and before I knew it, my two children had changed out of their Easter clothes into play clothes. Of course I didn't see them until everyone was gathered and ready to take the family photograph. By then, there wasn't time to get them dressed up again. I was tempted to get frustrated because, first of all, I wasn't finished showing them off in their Easter outfits, and second, we hadn't even taken pictures yet. In the family photo that year, everyone was dressed in their nice Easter clothes except my children. Today I would not trade that picture for anything; it is a family treasure. At the time, however, I couldn't see the big picture. All I could see was that my children were not wearing what I wanted them to wear in the photograph.

Sometimes we can look back on the things we thought were important but really didn't matter after all. We have to keep our eyes on the big picture so we don't miss the beauty of the moment. I'm sure my friend will look back on her vacation pictures thirty years from now and think, *Wow, I looked pretty good!*

Seeing the big picture can help us keep the right perspective. Today things may be difficult and seem like they are never going to get easier. Perhaps you feel like you are the only one facing your challenges. If you are not careful, you can become so absorbed in your own problems that you fall into a destructive cycle of self-pity. However, the truth is, many people would gladly exchange problems with you.

I heard about Linda, a young woman who seemed to have everything going for her. She had a great life, a thriving career, and a devoted circle of friends, but Linda wanted to lose the twenty-five pounds she had gained since her divorce two years earlier.

She tried just about everything she could, focusing on eating the right foods, drinking lots of water, and setting her alarm early enough that she could go to the gym at least three times a week. But all too frequently, she found herself sitting on her sofa with her two best friends — Ben and Jerry (Double Fudge Brownie, of course).

Linda decided to join a structured weight loss program that would keep her inspired and moving in the right direction. The night she arrived at her first meeting, she was both nervous and excited about the prospect of finding a solution to her all-consuming weight issue. "Finally! I can get rid of this weight and be happy," she said to herself. As she walked in, she saw an empty seat next to a woman wearing a long, casual dress. She introduced herself to the woman and began telling her how happy she expected to be when she lost her weight. Linda told the woman that she couldn't wait to wear a bathing suit again so she could water-ski at the lake and feel better about herself when working out at the gym. Realizing that she was dominating the conversation, Linda asked, "What made you decide to join the program?"

The woman replied, "Several years ago, I was in a terrible car accident and almost lost my life. I was so depressed after spending weeks in the hospital, all I could do was find comfort in food. Now I've gained so much weight that I can't wear the prosthetic leg I received after I lost my own leg in the accident. As soon as I get this weight off, I'm going to be able to fit into my prosthetic leg so I can walk again."

As Linda listened to the woman's story, her eyes welled with tears. At that moment, Linda decided to change her perspective. She determined first of all to help her newfound friend in any way she could. Second, she made the decision to start being more thankful and to focus on the blessings she had. Linda realized that she had allowed herself to become overwhelmed with her weight problem, which caused her to lose sight of the more important things in her life.

AVOID EXAGGERATED THINKING

We've all had seasons where we felt overwhelmed, and when that happens, it's easy for our thinking to get off track. One of the ways to find balance again is by learning to recognize and avoid exaggerated thinking. How can you identify exaggerated thinking in your own life? It often goes like this: "I'm never going to get a better job." "I'm never going to get married." "I'll always be in debt." "I'll never lose this weight." Sound familiar? Thinking in extremes narrows your focus. When we strive to keep a balanced perspective, we can see things for how they really are, manage life more easily, and find the solution to whatever it is we are facing. On the other hand, when exaggerated thinking creeps in, it can cause us to miss so many opportunities and important moments with family and loved ones.

One day Joel decided to take Alexandra on a father-daughter outing. They made plans to go to Build-A-Bear Workshop in the Galleria Mall and then have lunch. I kissed them good-bye and off they went. In little less than two hours, they were pulling back into the driveway, and I thought for sure that something was wrong. But then I saw the bear in Alexandra's arms, so I knew they had at least made it that far. When Alexandra came inside the house, I asked, "Did you and Daddy have a good time?"

"Yes," she gushed excitedly.

"Did you eat lunch?" I asked, thinking they'd be hungry.

"Oh, yes," Alexandra replied. "And Daddy took me to the candy store for my dessert."

I couldn't believe it. In my mind, the trip should have taken about four hours. If it were me, we would have spent at least an hour deciding which clothes to put on the bear; another hour or so at a cool restaurant, and then there's that cute little shoe store near the mall exit. I would have cleared my calendar for the whole afternoon. But in reality all my little daughter wanted to do was to spend some quality time with her daddy. After a short time, she was ready to come home anyway.

How often do we put off important things because we make them bigger in our minds than they really are? You can't do this or that because you think you need to schedule it far in advance, or you don't have the right clothes. Maybe you feel like you can't invite your family over because the dining room needs painting and the gutters need fixing. Or perhaps you think you can't have anyone over from the office because you think you must have perfect silverware, but the truth is, no one is going to remember the utensils with which they ate or how perfect your house was. What they will remember is the quality time spent with those who care about them.

How many moments do you miss because you are so wrapped up in making everything perfect? You obsess so much over your child's birthday party that you forget to stop and enjoy your own child, which is the whole point of the celebration. We've all been there, and most of the time, our frustration stems from our sincere desire to bless the people we love, but let's make sure we keep our perspective. Everything doesn't have to be perfect before you can enjoy life, and you don't have to take off an entire day to show someone that you care. Maybe all your child or loved one wants is for you to spread a blanket in the backyard and have a simple picnic. Sure, something will always come up, calling out for your immediate attention, but most things can wait. The laundry can wait, the phone can wait, the dishes can wait, but your loved ones need your investment of time and attention. Make your relationships a priority and find simple ways to enjoy the people you love. No one gets to the end of life and says, "Boy, I sure do wish I had worked more hours in the office," or, "I wish I would have had a cleaner house." No, at the end of their lives, most people say, "I wish I would have spent more time with my family and loved ones."

When it comes to facing challenges in relationships, our culture today makes it so easy to focus on momentary self-gratification rather than considering the long-term value of the investments made in those relationships. The most rewarding relationships are built and proven over time. It's similar to buying a house. Over time you build equity. If you had a beautiful house with $100,000 in equity, and then discovered a $2,500 plumbing problem, it may seem like a big deal, but compared to what you have invested, it's really a rather small problem. You wouldn't return your house keys to the bank over a $2,500 plumbing problem. It's easy to get bent out of shape over a problem like a leak in the roof, but that can be repaired. Instead, why not focus your energy on being thankful that you have a roof over your head?

In a similar manner, I encourage you to take a step back today and look at what you have invested in your relationships. Maybe you're facing some difficult times, but consider all you've come through so far. What's the value of the time, energy, heart, and commitment you've invested? Instead of focusing on the problems, choose to focus on the treasure of the relationship. When we get our perspective right regarding our relationships, those frustrations seem much more manageable.

One afternoon I was having a late lunch with a friend at a nice restaurant. Throughout the lunch I noticed my friend was becoming increasingly irritated with our waiter, who was somewhat forgetful, inattentive, and slow. I found the situation rather humorous and asked my friend why she was allowing the waiter to get her so annoyed. She told me, "I have a hard time dealing with people who take their time and are just plain slow. I get so frustrated when people are lollygagging around and halfway doing their job. I get so irritated sometimes that I blurt out something I know I shouldn't say. Then I get so mad at myself for doing that."

I could tell immediately that she needed to change her perspective, so I asked her, "What are you thinking about right now? Are you keeping score of his mistakes?"

She began to laugh and said, "Yes, that's exactly what I am doing."

Are you keeping score when you're at the grocery store checkout counter or sitting behind two cars at a slow drive-through? What's going through your mind when that coworker who seems to always annoy you approaches during lunch? Are you thinking, *Here we go again?* When you go back into your memory and retrieve past frustrations, you are setting yourself up to relive them.

I heard a story about a little girl who

whined and complained about everything one day. The next day she was cheerful and sweet to everyone. Her mother said, "Yesterday you had such a bad attitude. Today you're happy about everything. What happened?"

The little girl replied, "Yesterday my thoughts were pushing me around. Today I'm pushing my thoughts around."

We must take control of our thoughts; don't let the negative play over in your head and cause you to say and do things you will regret later. Instead of keeping score, keep a positive attitude. When it comes to those little irritations, let people off the hook by looking for the best in them.

I knew a couple who worked for the same company. They were in different departments and both loved their jobs until one day the husband encountered some situations that made him angry, and he ended up leaving the company. The wife was not involved in the trouble at all, but before long, his negativity about the company began to pollute her perspective. She began to imagine offenses that did not truly occur. She began seeing the company and her boss in a negative light. Sadly, it was not long before she quit the job she once loved.

Sometimes our attitude pollutes others

and we don't even know we are influencing them.

There was a husband and wife who were always talking negatively about his mother, not thinking about the fact that their four-year-old daughter was hearing everything they were saying. They assumed that because she was so young, it didn't matter, but whenever Grandma would come over, the little girl would pull back and try to hide. The couple had to urge their daughter to hug her grandma. Overhearing her parents' negative conversations affected the way she felt about her grandma.

Your words have power to influence other people. Don't sow discord among the people in your life. Instead, keep a positive perspective. See the best in them. When you magnify the good, then the good will increase. When you have a negative attitude, it not only makes it more difficult on you, but it makes life tougher on the people around you.

Having the right attitude and perspective means being flexible when things don't go the way you expect. The other day I was working in the living room while Alexandra was playing. I asked her for some water. She jumped up, ran into the kitchen, and came back with a glass half filled with water. She handed it to me and quickly went back to playing. I just chuckled to myself as I looked at the glass I was holding in my hand. I thought for a moment, *Life doesn't always give us what we are expecting.* Many times we get served half a glass of water, and we get to choose how we will respond. What's our perspective? I was expecting a full glass of water and my daughter's action — kind as it was — didn't meet my expectations. But I certainly had more water now than I had a few minutes earlier! Instead of getting upset about what I didn't have, I chose to be thankful for what I did have.

A positive person sees the best in every situation and uses her energy to bring solutions to life's challenges.

Did you know it takes more face muscles to frown than it does to smile? In the same way, it takes more energy to be negative than it does to be positive. When you have a positive attitude, you are cooperating with God.

Let me encourage you to get up every day and put on a fresh new attitude. Remember, these are the good old days! Make the most of this moment. If you'll keep the right perspective, approaching each day with faith, seeing the big picture, then I believe you can live life like the young woman in the commercial — strong, vibrant, positive, and hopeful.

ANCHOR THOUGHTS

I will not be consumed by my challenges. I will stay in faith, focus on the good, and keep the right perspective.

I choose to live this day happy, content, and grateful for what God has given me.

I will focus on what I have and not what I don't have. I will dwell on what's right in my life and magnify the good.

When things are difficult and I'm tempted to get discouraged, I will remember all the great things God has done in my past.

I recognize I was not created to constantly struggle and endure life. I am making a decision to celebrate each day, to live it to the full, and to enjoy the people in my life.

I will not long for the good old days, wishing it could be like it was. I realize today I've got great people in my life, great opportunities, and I'm making great memories. I know these are the good old days.

5

Making the Most of What You Have

When I was a young girl in elementary school, I had a shy personality, yet I always felt like there was something big inside me. I was a dreamer with a vivid imagination. When it came time for the fifth-grade school play, I really wanted the lead role; however, I didn't step up to make my teacher aware of it. The day came for the teacher to announce who would play the lead, and of course she didn't pick me, *the shy girl;* instead, she picked one of my classmates. Naturally I was disappointed, but even back then I was filled with hope and I imagined that somehow that little girl wouldn't be able to fulfill her role. Perhaps she would have to go out of town with her family, and there I would be, standing in the wings when my big moment came! The teacher would *have* to pick me after all. Yes, in my mind, I dreamed of getting the big part. Although it never happened, I rehearsed that scenario over and over in my mind, wishing I could play the lead.

Years later I realized that although I had been dreaming about playing the lead, I didn't take action. I didn't rehearse the lines or memorize the scenes. I didn't stay after school for the voluntary practices. Sure, I *desired* to play the role, but I certainly wasn't *preparing* for it. Had the teacher called on me, I wouldn't have been ready to walk through that door of opportunity, because I hadn't put action behind my dreams. Being filled with hope and expectation is a great place to start, but it's also a poor place to stop.

How often do we "sit in the wings" of life, wishing we were doing more, believing that we have more in us, waiting for our big moment? Yet if opportunity were to knock on our door, we might not even be ready. If you are really believing and expecting that big things will happen, you have to put action behind your faith and live your life ready to make the most of every opportunity. I've heard it said that *success happens when preparation meets opportunity.* That's why it is important to use and develop your gifts and talents so when opportunity presents itself, you will have the confidence to walk through those open doors.

Life is lived one day at a time, and the way to prepare for tomorrow is to live at your very best today. Whether you want to further your career or change some bad habits, if you'll do what you know how to do today, God will help you get to where you need to be tomorrow. Don't fall into the trap of thinking, *When my boss recognizes my talent, then I will start doing my best work,* or, *As soon as I get another job, then I will be happy.* Or perhaps, *When my children grow up, then I can pursue my dreams.* No, don't put your life on hold until the *big moment;* start today. Take some classes, expand your horizons, do your best whether your boss praises you or not. Every day lived well is one day closer to accomplishing your dreams. Start using what you have and doing what you know how to do, and God will open the door to new opportunity.

LOOK FOR SUCCESS IN EVERY DAY

It's important to look for success in every day. Maybe things weren't perfect today, maybe you cheated on your diet or said something you wish you hadn't, but thank God you realized it and are now taking steps in the right direction. Don't focus on your mistakes; focus on your milestones. Maybe you've made some wrong decisions, but you've made a whole lot of right decisions, too. Maybe you didn't get everything done you wanted to do, but at least you've gotten some things accomplished. You're better off than you were in your past and your future is getting brighter and brighter. See yourself as successful, because what you set your focus on will become reality.

The Scripture says, "To those who have, more will be given."[11] That means you will tap into more gifts, talents, and opportunities as you continue to use what you have been given. Jesus told a story about a wealthy man who entrusted some of his money, called *talents* in those days, to three of his employees. He instructed them to invest the talents and make the most of what he gave them while he was gone. On his return, he found that two of the men used their talents wisely and doubled the return on their investments. However, one man said, "I buried my talent because I was afraid." He was full of excuses, trying to explain why he didn't do anything constructive with what he was given. Perhaps he thought he didn't have any good contacts or maybe he was taking care of other issues. Regardless, the wealthy man asked, "Couldn't you have at least put my money in a savings account so it could draw interest?" The employer was so frustrated that he took what he had given him and gave it to the first man who had been faithful.[12]

It's interesting that *all* of the men had the same opportunity, but the man full of excuses didn't take advantage of it.

That's the way God works. He has entrusted every person with a measure of gifts, talents, and abilities. He's watching to see what we will do with them. If you are faithful with what God has given you, He will multiply your gifts and increase them in ways you never dreamed. It's not about how much you have; it is about *using* what you have. Don't allow excuses to cause you to bury what you have been given. Just as the wealthy man wasn't moved by excuses, God is not moved by excuses either. He is moved by our faith. So make the decision to wake up every day and look for ways to use what God has placed in your hands. Believe in yourself and believe that God is working on your behalf. It may not happen tomorrow, or next week, but if you will stay in faith, you will grow and increase.

Sometimes opportunities come our way and we think, *I can't do that,* or, *That's impossible.* We make so many excuses that we eventually start living those excuses as if they were the truth and we never even attempt to explore other possibilities.

One day I was having a conversation with a friend who was encouraging me to do a particular thing, and before I even thought twice about it, I blurted out, "Oh, I can't do that!" It wasn't because I didn't *want* to do it; I had just made excuses about doing that for so long, I had convinced myself that I couldn't do it. Later on, I thought to myself, *Why can't I do that? I* can *do that.* I realized I had basically hung a DO NOT ENTER sign at the door of that area. I didn't even stop to consider the reasons I could do it. All I saw was DO NOT ENTER.

Have you ever heard yourself say, "I can't do that; I am not that talented; I don't have the finances," or, "I haven't done that in so long, I am too old; I am too out of shape"? If you have, you might need to check for a DO NOT ENTER sign in your own thinking! It's easy to think, *I'm never going to get married. I've been single for too long.* Or you think, *I'm never going to get out of debt. I owe too much and can't seem to get ahead.* Don't allow yourself to make excuses, because if you make them long enough, you may start to believe them yourself.

Keep God's promises in the forefront of your thinking. Have the attitude "I may not have met the right person yet, but I know he is out there. I'm going to focus my efforts on *being* the right kind of person so when God opens that door, I will be ready." Or say, "I may not see how I could ever get out of debt, but I know God says I am blessed, and as I do my part, God will help me." Maybe you are saying, "I have been overweight for so long I could never look like I did when I got married." Take down that DO NOT ENTER sign; go back and try again! Keep a good attitude, write God's promises in your heart, and you will see great things in your life!

Moses had a DO NOT ENTER sign in his mind. When God called him to lead the Hebrew people out of captivity, the first statement out of Moses' mouth was "I can't God; I stutter."[13] Moses wanted to help the Israelites, but he'd made so many excuses that he didn't believe in himself. But God wanted to help Moses. He wanted to empower him, so He told Moses, "I will send your brother, Aaron, to help you."

Just as God helped Moses, He wants to help you accomplish great things in your life, too. If you will take down the DO NOT ENTER signs and try again, God will help you. He will bring the right people across your path and open new doors in front of you.

Sometimes God presents opportunities that look small, or insignificant, maybe even ordinary. Perhaps you don't see how they fit into the big picture of your life. However, if God is presenting you with something, He has a purpose for it and He can increase you and promote you to larger responsibilities.

For many years, Joel's father had a hair stylist who would help him with his hair and make sure he looked his best before he ministered. One day she wasn't able to do it anymore, and I happened to be standing there when she announced her resignation. Joel's father immediately turned to me and asked if I would take her place. Now, I wasn't a hairdresser. I didn't go to cosmetology school. My first thought was, *If you're bold enough to trust me, I'm bold enough to do it. It's your hair!* Even though I didn't feel qualified, I remembered that I did have *some* experience. Though I would never list it on a résumé, when I was a young girl, maybe thirteen or fourteen years old, my friends in the neighborhood would come over and we would go out to the garage and I would cut their hair. And what started as simple haircuts turned to coloring and highlights. I practically had my own neighborhood beauty shop right in the garage.

Joel's father used to tell us he was going to be preaching into his nineties, and I had no reason to believe any different. I remember one day I was calculating how old I would be and still doing Daddy's hair when he was ninety; and I can tell you it would have been a long time! Nevertheless, I was committed. I told God, "If this is what You have for me to do, I am going to be the most faithful person You can find. I am going to stick with this even when there are many other things I would like to be doing."

It was difficult to see how this fit into the big picture of my life or where this could possibly take me. But when I didn't understand, one scriptural principle always came to my heart and mind: If you will be faithful in the little things, God will trust you with much more.

God needs us to pass the faithfulness test so He can pour into us greater things. Are you being responsible for what's in your hands right now? If you want to grow and increase in any area of your life, you have to use what you have been given; then God will multiply it. If you want to grow in discipline, start being on time everywhere you go. If you want to get in better physical shape, take a walk for some exercise. If you want that promotion at work, do your best at your current job, and God will increase you. Don't wait around for the big moment. If you have a gift to sing, don't wait around for Sony Records to sign you to a contract; sing in your church choir. You never know what door God will open for you as you begin to use what you have.

As I look back over my time with Daddy Osteen, or "The Big O," as I used to call him, I wouldn't trade that experience for anything. I loved him and he loved me. We had a bond that I will always cherish. I believe if it were not for those years we spent together, I would not have the same opportunities I have today. When you are faithful to God, He will be faithful to you.

There's an old story about a traveler who hiked for many miles across the desert. His water supply was gone, and he knew that if he didn't find water soon, he would surely die. In the distance, he noticed an abandoned cabin and hoped to find some water there. Once he made it to the cabin, he discovered an old well. Then he noticed a tin can tied to the pump, with a note inside. The note said:

Dear stranger:

This water pump is in working condition, but the pump needs to be primed in order for the water to come out. Under the white rock, I buried a jar of water, out of the sun. There's enough water in the jar to prime the pump, but not if you drink any first. When you are finished, please fill the jar and put it back as you found it for the next stranger who comes this way.

Just like this hiker, sometimes you have to be willing to pour in everything you have before you can see God's increase flowing in your life. You have to be willing to trust that you can tap into His deep, abundant supply of resources. I encourage you to give God what you have in your hands today, and as you stay faithful to do your part, God will do His part. It takes faith and courage to "prime your pump," but remember, God has already given you what you need to take the first step. When you put action behind your faith and trust God, He will pour wisdom, strength, and creativity into you and help you accomplish the dreams and desires He has placed in your heart.

Joel has always been the type of person to give 100 percent to whatever he is doing, so it was no different when he started the television ministry. He was just nineteen years old, but he had passion, knowledge, perseverance, and discipline. He poured in everything he had, because he believed that's what God wanted him to do. He worked with excellence, and as the years went by, the ministry began to grow. Joel remained faithful through the years, always giving his very best. When we redesigned the platform area where his father spoke each week, he paid careful attention to every little detail — from the height of the podium to even the smallest adjustments in the lighting. Every day he lived and worked at his best and those small steps carried him to where he is today.

Joel's greatest strength was his dedication, not only in doing the small things, but he was dedicated to growing and expanding his vision. I remember one time he had lined up some radio programs and special events for his father. Joel had so much creativity and energy; he was so excited to bring new opportunities to his father. One day he was presenting some of his ideas and his father lovingly told him, "Joel, I am seventy-five years old, and I don't want to do all these new projects you are giving me. All I want to do is pastor the church and continue the weekly television program."

I remember how disappointed Joel was, but as he repeated that conversation to me, one thing he said was "My father founded this church, and *whether I agree with every decision or not,* I am going to remain faithful to him." Joel had plenty of opportunities to do exciting television programs in different countries, but he chose to remain faithful where he was. Day in and day out, he edited his father's program and kept developing the gifts and talents God gave him. Now we realize those seventeen years behind the scenes were a time of testing. God was testing Joel's faithfulness and allowing him to prove himself. God was seeing what Joel was able to handle. Even when it wasn't exciting, even when he didn't get his way, Joel stuck with it and did his job with excellence, to the best of his ability. Today God is bringing out those deeper talents on the inside of Joel, increasing him and giving him more opportunity.

That's what God wants to do in your life. He wants to bring out talents you didn't even know you had. He wants to give you greater opportunities than you ever dreamed. You have so much untapped talent and potential on the inside — gifts, creativity, ideas. But those treasures will lie dormant for a lifetime — just like the water in that well — unless you are willing to take what you have and prime the pump. Use your gifts and put your faith into action. If you have a desire in your heart to teach or minister, start with the children's ministry at your church. You may say, "Oh, I'm made for more than teaching children." Maybe so, but if you'll be faithful with little and do your best, you're sowing a seed. You're giving God something to multiply, and at the right time, He'll open up bigger and better doors.

When our son, Jonathan, was just a little boy, he loved attending children's church, and it was because of Mr. Ed. No, we didn't have a talking horse at the church. Mr. Ed was one of the volunteers — a talented professional artist who used the gifts that God gave him to draw Bible characters and tell stories to help teach the Scriptures to children in a fun, relevant way. His drawings were so good and so effective that Jonathan often asked if he could take them home. Mr. Ed had a profound impact on our son and the other children he taught, and we are grateful. Even though he was amazingly talented, he never once gave the impression that teaching children was beneath him. He gave those kids his very best.

As you impart good things into the lives of other people, God will impart good things into your life. When you give what you have in your hand, it doesn't matter how small you think it is, God can bless it and God can multiply it.

One time Jesus was preaching to a large crowd on the side of a hill. People traveled a long way to hear Him teach and they were starting to get hungry. Of course there wasn't a McDonald's or a Domino's delivery anywhere. The disciples urged Jesus to send the crowds away so they could travel back to find food before it got dark. But Jesus said, "I'm not going to turn them away; I'm going to feed them."[14]

He used the lunch of a small boy, two fish and five small loaves of bread, and multiplied it and fed thousands of people that day.

Sometimes what you have seems small. It may only look like five loaves and two fish in comparison to what you need, but don't limit God the way the disciples did. Nothing is too small in His eyes. His resources are not limited to what you have. He is the source of all things, and His supply is limitless. Give Him what is in your hands, and allow Him to multiply it.

The more we use our God-given potential, the more fulfilled and the happier we will be. It's not always easy to step through a door of opportunity, but sometimes we just have to be bold and go for it. It's sort of like getting into a cold swimming pool on a warm day; it's a lot easier if you just jump right in! When an opportunity shows up, and you know it is right for you, don't let fear hold you back. You can't give yourself time to reason it all out, because you might talk yourself right out of it. You'll think of every excuse in the world to stay where you are. But remember, if God gives you the opportunity, He has already given you the ability to accomplish it. Don't be afraid of more responsibility.

That's the way I felt when I began speaking at Lakewood. I didn't give myself time to reason it all out in my mind, because I knew I would talk myself out of it. Instead of thinking about all the reasons that I couldn't do it, I started thinking about all the reasons that I *could* do it. I encouraged myself and allowed the Word of God to empower me. And yes, I was scared! But I knew that God wanted me to step into my position and begin to encourage people. So I took a step of faith and He was right there with me. Now I am only half scared. The truth is, I pressed through and gained ground. The more I did it, the easier it became. That is exactly what God wants for you. He wants you to overcome your fear and do what He has called you to do. What is in your hands may seem small, but don't put limits on what God can do with it.

I know now, if I would have talked myself out of speaking at Lakewood I would have breezed right by the door God had opened for me. Had I just sat in the wings, I can tell you, I would not be writing this book, and experiencing the satisfaction and fulfillment I have today.

Let me encourage you, don't shrink back and hide your talent, and don't let excuses keep you from God's best. He wants you to live a fulfilled and rewarding life. Take down the DO NOT ENTER signs and open your mind to the possibilities. God is always placing new opportunities in your path. Whether small or large, be faithful. Do your best with what you have. Every day you go out and give it your all is a day you're passing the test. God is keeping the records. He's the one who brings promotion. Even when it seems small, you don't know what it's going to lead to. It may not look like your big moment, but it can lead to your big moment. Remember, it's not about how much you have. The real question is: Are you using what you have? Make the most of your opportunities. Get prepared. If you'll do all you can do, God will do what you can't do. He'll open up the right doors and you'll fulfill the dreams He's placed in your heart.

ANCHOR THOUGHTS

I will live my life one day at a time knowing that I'm preparing for tomorrow by living my very best today.

I will be faithful with the talent, time, and opportunity God has given me. I realize that when I make the most of what I have, God will multiply it and give me more.

I will meditate on God's promises, keeping my mind filled with thoughts of hope, faith, and victory.

I will invest in the lives of those around me — encouraging my family, being good to my friends, helping those in need. I believe that as I bless others, God will bless me.

I will not shrink back in fear or be intimidated about doing what God has put in my path. I will be bold and courageous. I will take steps of faith and make the most of every opportunity.

I recognize that God has given me everything I need for the future. I have the talent, the wisdom, and the strength to fulfill my destiny.

Today I will do everything I can do, knowing that God will do what I can't do.

6
Recovering Lost Opportunities

When I look back over my life, I can see where I've missed out on some God-given opportunities. Maybe you are saying the same thing. If so, I want to encourage you: Don't live in regret. Don't let lost opportunities make you feel disappointed and discouraged. God is bigger than your lost opportunities. He can still get you where you need to go in life.

Have you ever used one of those GPS directional systems in your car? You set the location where you want to go, and the GPS calculates the best route. You can be driving along and get distracted and completely miss the street where the GPS instructed you to turn, but that doesn't mean you'll never reach your destination. That GPS system will instantly recalculate the route, based on your present location. God works in a similar way. He is constantly giving us direction, speaking to our hearts, leading us by granting peace or unrest in our spirit, but even when we miss His instructions — and we all do from time to time — He will recalculate our route and get us back where we need to be.

I love what the Apostle Paul said: "This one thing I do; forgetting those things which are behind, I reach forth to the things which are before me."[15] He was saying that we must turn our thoughts toward the present and future and keep looking for the new opportunities in our paths. Be prepared, because God is ready to fulfill the dreams and desires He's placed within your heart. He loves to restore opportunities that once seemed lost forever. And sometimes He brings those opportunities back in ways we haven't considered or weren't looking for. It may not always be the way we thought; but if you'll stay open, God will bless you beyond your wildest dreams.

One Christmas several years ago, I was longing to do something special for God. I began thinking of all the women in shelters and homes around the city and I felt a strong desire to make some Christmas baskets, filling them full of perfume and toiletries, and taking them to a women's shelter. I was excited about my idea and I searched through the yellow pages to find a nearby shelter. When I dialed the number, a woman answered, and I immediately began sharing my heart, telling her what I wanted to do, and how I hoped to make the women at the shelter feel special. But rather than getting excited with me and giving me the information I needed, she began to grill me with questions. She said, "This is a private facility and the women need to remain anonymous." Then she asked, "Have you been abused? Do you know somebody who has been abused? Do you need help, are you looking for help?"

"No," I said. "I just want to brighten the day for some women." She went on and on as though she hadn't even heard me, apparently thinking that I was trying to disguise some abuse that I had suffered. Finally I ended the conversation and hung up the phone in frustration. I thought to myself, *I'll call back tomorrow and speak to someone else.* But as life would have it, I became busy with family holiday projects, and before I knew it, the holidays were whizzing by and I had missed the opportunity.

A few days after the holidays had ended, I was praying when I thought about the Christmas baskets and the opportunity I had allowed to slip away. I told God that I felt I had lost my determination and had let those women down somehow. I asked Him to present another opportunity to me and I promised that this time I would see it through.

Several months went by, and then one day I received a telephone call from The Bridge, a women's shelter in Houston similar to the one I had contacted. A woman named Jackie was on the other end of the phone line. "Hi, Victoria, I'm the director of The Bridge," she told me, "and I attend Lakewood Church. I want to invite you to speak at my Women of Distinction Awards program. It's a benefit for the women's shelter." She told me about the event and who would be there — city leaders, business leaders, and others. Clearly she was so happy and proud of this event. As she was speaking, I thought about those Christmas baskets I had wanted to make for the women's shelter several months earlier, as well as the prayer. I was honored by her request, and I immediately said yes. When I hung up the phone, I thought, *Oh, God, those Christmas baskets would have been so much easier! Couldn't I have just started there?* At the time I didn't have experience speaking in front of large audiences. I had butterflies in my stomach just thinking about it! But, even though I was nervous about the speaking engagement, I felt this was the opportunity I had prayed for.

I worked so hard to prepare my presentation and rehearsed what I would say, practicing over and over in my mind. After the event, I felt I had done the best I could and I was happy about what I had accomplished and what I had experienced that day. Following my speech, I was elated when several of the attendees congratulated me, telling me how inspiring my talk had been to them. Later I was told that a professional athlete and his wife were so moved by my presentation that they made a large donation to the shelter. I was so encouraged.

It took faith and work, but it was marvelous to see how God brought back an opportunity I had missed.

I know God can do something similar for you. Everyone has missed opportunities to do something good, to help somebody, or even to go to the next level in our career. For one reason or another, we've allowed that opportunity to slip through our fingers. But let bygones be bygones; don't get trapped in the past. Don't allow yourself to focus on the things you've missed or could have done better. Allow Him to bring back any opportunities that you may have missed.

Joel's sister, Lisa, and her husband, Kevin,

tried for years to have children, but Lisa was not able to conceive. She went through all the fertility treatments and even several surgeries, but still no baby. Finally the doctor told Lisa there was nothing more he could do; they weren't going to be able to have children. Lisa and Kevin were devastated. It looked like their dreams had died, but God always has a plan. One day out of the blue Lisa received a call from Nancy Alcorn of Mercy Ministries, a home for at-risk young women based in Nashville.

"Lisa, I normally wouldn't do this," Nancy said, "but we have a young woman who is about to give birth to twin girls, and we were wondering if you and Kevin might be interested in adopting them."

Lisa and Kevin had not yet considered adoption since they were still hoping to have children naturally, but suddenly Lisa's interest was piqued.

"There's only one problem," Nancy said. "I know you and Kevin have most of the qualifications that the birth mother wants for the adoptive parents, but she also has a stipulation that her babies should be placed in a family with twins in their background."

Nancy had no idea that Kevin had a twin sister, and as soon as she said that, something inside Lisa's heart confirmed this was a "God opportunity." A few months later, Lisa and Kevin adopted those twin baby girls, and then three years later, they adopted another "Mercy" baby boy.

God gave Lisa and Kevin three children they could not have had naturally. Their hearts were open for what God wanted to do in their lives even though it wasn't the way they first anticipated. God gave them another opportunity to be the parents they desired to be. They could have just as easily given up and closed their minds, but they didn't. They remained open and God brought back that opportunity in a different way. Lisa will tell you, "These children came straight from my heart. I couldn't have had better children!"

I believe God is saying to us today, "I can restore the years that you've lost." Things may not have gone your way in the past and you think your dreams have died, but God has new opportunities in front of you. He wants the rest of your life to be better than ever.

One day I received a letter from a woman named Micki McHay; her husband had passed away and she was distraught and brokenhearted. She described how she couldn't see how she could make it through such a painful experience. She began to pray and ask God to help her. One night she was reading my husband Joel's book and she came across the statement "When one dream dies, dream another dream." Those words touched her heart. She thought about a children's book and music CD she had started to write many years before, but had never finished it. That night, faith was reignited in her heart. She felt God was opening another door in her life. She made a decision that she was going to pick up where she left off and pursue her dream. She found an illustrator, and before long, she released *The Ugly Snowflake,* a delightful children's book about a little snowflake that discovered her true, unique beauty.

That letter was accompanied by an autographed copy of the book and CD, which my young daughter asked me to read to her over and over again.

Not only did God rebirth a dream in Micki McHay's heart that night, but also He is using it to bless and encourage the lives of children everywhere.

Maybe you've gone through a loss and it looks like a dream has died, but if you'll search your heart and dare to dream another dream, you can see great days up ahead. If there are things in your heart that you have laid down for one reason or another, ask

God to give you another opportunity and open your heart and mind to His possibilities.

One day Joel and I were sitting together looking at pictures of our children when they were young, and we were enjoying the memories. As we reminisced over photos of Alexandra when she was in the little princess stage, I said to Joel, "Aren't these pictures beautiful? Remember when we had those princess birthday parties, and everything was pink?"

Joel's face looked puzzled. "You know, Victoria, I don't really remember that. I know I must have been there, but I don't have a strong memory of those times."

As Joel and I talked about it, we realized that he didn't have the same memories of Alexandra's early childhood as he did of Jonathan's. Alexandra was a newborn when Joel's father passed away. We were thrust into leading Lakewood Church, and we were doing our best just to stay afloat.

Overnight, Joel's responsibilities increased a hundredfold. Everyone was vying for his time and he was being pulled in every direction. The church was growing at an astonishing rate and the pressure on him was enormous. On top of all that, he was preaching on TV to millions of people, all of whom had come to expect a masterpiece each week. For the first three years of his ministry, Joel's mind was consumed by the awesome responsibility into which he had been thrust. No wonder Joel had a hard time remembering those early years in Alexandra's life.

Joel and I prayed that God would make up for that lost opportunity. Today Joel makes every effort to be the best dad to his little girl. He takes time for his children and today Alexandra and Joel's relationship is as close as close can be. Alexandra loves to do everything with her daddy. They play outside together, even go to the mall together. Alexandra is "Daddy's girl."

Maybe you feel like you weren't as good a parent as you should have been. Perhaps you were busy just trying to keep your head above water, and consequently, your relationships with your family members are not what they should be. You may be tempted to feel guilty and think, *If only I had spent more time with them and made them a higher priority.* Fretting over missed opportunities won't help. However, you can ask God to give you another chance. Pray that He will show you how to reach out to that person and make up for lost time. Be open for a new way to connect with the people in your life. When you are open and look for creative ways to communicate with the people in your life, God will help you.

We've all missed good chances, but ultimately, you'll never fail unless you quit.

For me, that telephone call inviting me to speak at the benefit for the women's shelter not only opened an opportunity to serve, but it stretched me to a new level. It increased my realm of influence and opened the door to relationships that I will forever cherish. I would have been so happy making those Christmas baskets, but God enabled me to minister in a completely new way.

You may be thinking you've wasted years of your life in the wrong career or associating with the wrong people, but God is saying, "I can restore those years." You may think that it's been too long, you've been through too much, and you're never going to see those new seasons of increase. But the same God who gave Lisa and Kevin three beautiful children can make up for lost time for you. Why don't you ask God to give you back every opportunity that you've missed? He may not always do so in the way you are expecting, but open your heart and mind to the possibilities. Be ready to embrace the opportunities God will bring across your path. As you do, you'll rise higher and higher and you will Love Your Life the way God intends.

ANCHOR THOUGHTS

I believe God is bigger than my lost opportunities and today He is restoring dreams, plans, and goals that I allowed to pass by.

I will not live in negativity and disappointment because of failures and setbacks. One dream may have died, but today I am dreaming a new dream.

Even though it looks like I may have wasted years of my life in the wrong career, a failed relationship, or unhealthy environment, I'm choosing to stay in faith, knowing that God can restore those years to me.

I will not focus on what I lost or what I missed out on; I know God can resurrect dead dreams and He still has a way to bring them about.

7
OVERCOMING OFFENSES

My entire life, my family has been in the jewelry business. I grew up in the jewelry store, helping my mother and waiting on customers from the time I was in elementary school. Over the years, I've learned quite a bit about gemstones and precious metals, but the story of the pearl has always fascinated me.

Most people know that a pearl comes from an oyster. It isn't just luck of the draw or random chance — in fact, that little oyster has to do a lot of work and endure quite a bit of hardship during the making of that pearl. And the most amazing part of the process is that the oyster's goal isn't even to make a pearl. The oyster's goal is to insulate itself from the offending irritant.

A pearl is formed when a single grain of sand or a tiny foreign particle is lodged inside an oyster. If left alone, that tiny particle will cause damage to the tender mollusk. The particle is an irritant, causing the oyster to produce a lacquer-like substance called nacre. The oyster secretes the nacre to cover that irritant as a means of protecting itself. It constantly works to shield itself from the irritant. Those layers of nacre coat the sand granule, eventually sealing away the irritation and forming a gorgeous pearl.

Offenses are just like that grain of sand — when someone says or does something to us that offends us, it is as if they put sand in our oyster. While the oyster always knows how to deal with its grain of sand, we too need to learn how to deal with the offenses that irritate us.

Throughout our lives, unfair things will happen. People will let us down, they'll say things that hurt our feelings, and they won't always treat us the way we think they should. If we allow those offenses to take root in our heart, they will cause us to become bitter and lose our joy and enthusiasm for life. We must learn to insulate ourselves from offenses and to keep our hearts pure. One of the keys to loving your life is learning how to take those negative things, give them to God, and allow Him to produce the priceless pearls our lives are meant to be.

I have a friend who is a beautiful, talented, vibrant woman. She has a vivacious, upbeat personality and is always full of enthusiasm and life. That's just who she is — positive and passionate. But not everyone embraces her positive personality. One day at work as she entered the boardroom for an early morning meeting, she overheard a few of her coworkers talking about her. They said, "She is just so over the top all the time. Sometimes I want to say to her, 'Are you for real?' Oh, no. Here she comes. I just don't know if I can take her perkiness this morning."

My friend didn't say anything at the time, but those words really wounded her heart. It was as if they had poured a bucket of sand in her oyster. Instead of going into that meeting with her positive attitude and sparkling personality, she quietly took her seat and remained withdrawn for the entire meeting. She began doubting herself and tried to adjust her personality to counteract the words she overheard that day.

Shortly thereafter, she joined me and a group of our friends for lunch. I noticed right away that she was quiet and sullen, so I asked her what was wrong. After a moment of hesitation, she told us what had happened in the meeting. She said she was going to tone down her personality so she would be more accepted by the other women in the office. I listened for a while, and then I said to her, "Are you kidding me? You are one of the brightest, most outgoing, wonderful women I know! Your personality is great and you can use it to influence a lot of people for good. Don't change who you are simply because your coworkers can't appreciate your gifts!" Everyone at the table agreed and began telling her how much they appreciated and enjoyed her vivacious personality.

Immediately my friend realized that she was letting her coworkers' disapproval cause her to doubt herself and negatively affect her self-esteem. As far as she and I are concerned, she is the beautiful pearl among the grains of sand in her office.

Do you ever find that you do something similar? Maybe someone in your life has said hurtful things about your personality, your appearance, or your abilities and you've altered yourself for their approval. Understand, just because somebody says something about you, doesn't make it true. Just as I told my friend, I'm telling you today: You are created in the image of Almighty God and He gave you the gifts and personality you have for a purpose. You may not be like everyone else, but that's okay. Be who God made you to be and do not be defined by the opinions of other people.

Alexandra loves gymnastics. She loves to do back bends, cartwheels, twists, and turns. She is always saying, "Mommy, watch this," as she tries something new. I remember when she began learning how to do one-handed cartwheels. She spent a day or two practicing them in the living room and then I noticed that she began doing something else. I asked her how her cartwheel was coming along and if she would do one for me. To my complete surprise, she declined; in fact, I could tell that my request bothered her. I asked her why she didn't want to do one for me. "Mom," she said hesitantly, "Curtis told me I wasn't good at it, and he made fun of me. So I am going to learn to do a roundabout instead." Curtis was one of the boys in her class at school — and at that very moment one of my least favorite.

I thought for a moment and then asked, "Oh! Is Curtis a cartwheel expert?"

She looked at me, slightly perplexed, and then answered, "No."

"Perhaps he is an Olympic gymnast?" I asked.

"No!" she said. I could tell she was beginning to understand my point.

"Well then, he must surely be a gymnastics expert of some kind."

By now, a smile was on her face. "Mom, you know he is not an expert in cartwheels!"

"Well then, do you believe you are not good at cartwheels just because Curtis told you so?" I asked.

Alexandra completely understood what I was telling her. We talked a little bit more about it, she did half a dozen cartwheels for me, and then I kissed her brightened little face. As I turned to go into the kitchen, I heard her begin to sing an old rhyme: "I am rubber, you are glue; whatever you say bounces off me and sticks to you!"

I laughed at her sweet, innocent perspective, and then I thought, *There's a lot of truth to that old rhyme.* If we could only get that down into our hearts as adults, it would serve us well! Certainly we should always consider the constructive opinions of people we respect, but don't let anyone's words alter your personality or deter you from using your gifts and talents. Just because someone criticizes you, doesn't make it true. Don't let the words of others define you; instead, insulate that offense. Let it bounce right off you.

Don't Let Offenses Hang Around

One thing I find interesting about the oyster is that it doesn't let much time pass before it begins to cover the grain of sand with nacre. It doesn't let the sand linger at all. There is a very good lesson in that for all of us. If we allow offenses to hang around they will cause damage that can be nearly impossible to reverse. The results can be devastating.

Two sisters, Shelly and Susan, have been friends of our family for many years. Several years ago, they shared a traumatic experience when their mother went through a prolonged illness and eventually died. Up until that time, Shelly and Susan had been very close, and at first they rallied together and found comfort in each other. That is, until it came time to deal with their mother's rather modest estate, which consisted of a small house, some furniture, and about $50,000 in life insurance. Their mother's will provided for each of the daughters to receive an equal share.

Shortly after the funeral, Shelly, Susan, and Susan's husband, Tom, were sitting in Shelly's dining room discussing whether they were going to sell the house or rent it. Tom suddenly blurted out, "You know, Shelly, your mother always loved you the most, and it seems that Susan should get the house just to even things out!"

Shelly was floored and hardly knew what to say to Tom when she noticed that Susan was nodding her head in agreement. "Susan, why are you nodding your head?" she asked. Susan looked at Tom, then back at Shelly, and then began to tell Shelly that she had always felt that way. "You were Mom's little princess," she told Shelly. "You could do no wrong." Susan then spent the next ten minutes telling Shelly how much she resented her for that. As you might imagine, the conversation became a heated argument filled with accusations and offenses. Finally, Susan and Tom stormed out of the house, got into their car, and sped away.

The next afternoon Shelly received a notice from Susan's attorney informing her that Susan was contesting their mother's will. Now Shelly was offended as well, and she became angry at Susan. She picked up the phone and called a friend, who referred her to an attorney.

A year and a half later, the case was settled. The house was sold to pay attorney's fees and each of the sisters received about $25,000 — well short of what they could have received had they not allowed their offenses to devastate their relationship. The saddest part of this tale is that they have not spoken to each other since that day in Shelly's dining room.

As a family, they were torn apart by lingering offenses. The entire episode could have been avoided had Susan confided in her sister and dealt with her negative feelings years earlier instead of allowing the bitterness and resentment to grow in her heart.

We have to recognize when our thinking is moving in the wrong direction. If we are not careful, we will get wrapped up in our own self-pity and despair. If we dwell on those thoughts long enough, we will take ownership of destructive attitudes that will distract our thinking and hinder our life. If we don't deal with the little things in our lives, they'll become big things and rob us of the rich, fruitful life God has in store.

It is important to realize that offenses can be like a seed that will take root and begin to grow. I remember one time early in our marriage Joel and I were having a disagreement. There was no way that we were going to see eye to eye, my feelings were hurt, and I was highly frustrated. Joel, on the other hand, didn't see our disagreement as a big deal and had grown tired of talking about it. So to placate me and end the discussion, he halfheartedly said, "I'm sorry." That was good enough for him and he went about his business. But as I walked into the other room, behind the closed door, I turned around and stuck out my tongue out at him. It seemed innocent enough, but even through my frustration with him, I knew it was disrespectful. After a few minutes of contemplation, I realized that I couldn't let that disrespect take root in my heart. I had to deal with it quickly. So I went into the kitchen, found Joel, and told him that even though he was wrong, I loved him and respected him. Joel simply smiled and said, "I knew you would come around."

I really believe that if you start showing disrespect even in small ways, soon it will manifest itself into larger displays of disrespect that can damage a good relationship. When you allow offenses to linger and grow, before long they will become big issues that strain and weaken relationships. I recognized that the gesture of sticking out my tongue — as innocuous as it may have been — was planting seeds of resentment in my own heart, and I didn't want to reap that kind of harvest in our relationship. Now I'm careful to let those things go and not allow them to linger in my heart.

HEALING THROUGH A PURE HEART

So often people hold on to bitterness or resentment, thinking that they are stockpiling ammunition against the person who hurt or offended them; as if one day they'll have the chance to get even. Or perhaps they are holding on to the evidence because they think they're waiting for their day in emotional court. However, the truth is, if you don't choose to forgive, the only person being punished is you! Unforgiveness is like a barrier that actually blocks the door to your heart. We must remove the barrier, fling open the door, and extend forgiveness to others. When your heart is open, you can then release all the hurt and pain and make room for God's healing.

I heard a story about a woman in her mid-thirties who had an abusive, tumultuous marriage. Her husband was a heavy drinker; he had several affairs and finally abandoned her and her three young children. Understandably, she had many worries and concerns that were consuming her life. It was as if the weight of the world was on her shoulders and she felt completely overwhelmed. She felt betrayed, angry, and hurt, not to mention under financial pressure. At night, she'd lay awake imagining confrontations with her former husband. She would play in her mind over and over all of the offenses and wrongs that he had committed against her; she wanted so badly to get even.

It was the most difficult time in her life. She got to the point where she didn't want to face the day. She was so discouraged that all she wanted to do was pull the covers over her head and stay in bed. The only solace she could find was her faith in God. One night while she was praying, she realized she had to do something. She knew she had to change her perspective and find a way to keep moving forward. She had three beautiful children depending on her and her whole life ahead of her. She knew that the longer she stayed in that despair, the deeper she would sink. She cried out, "God, you've got to help me. I can't go on like this. I can't take care of my children. Please help me forgive." She realized it was going to be an act of her will.

She came up with a way to visualize those burdens being released. She imagined herself holding a bouquet of helium-filled balloons and each one represented a specific offense, worry, concern, or care. She stretched out her arm and one at a time released the balloons and watched them float away. She said, "God, I'm giving you this pain and unforgiveness right now. I'm releasing this to you." She stood there and watched it rise up to the heavens. She took the next balloon and said, "Father, all the doubt, all the insecurities about my future, I'm releasing it to you right now." As she did this, she could literally feel the weight of those offenses, cares, and concerns that had consumed her began to lift off her. Her spirit began to breathe in hope. Faith began to fill her heart. She felt a new strength come into her body.

Every morning she continued to release her balloons, not allowing herself to be overwhelmed by her responsibilities and consumed by the hurts of the past. As she did, she received a fresh portion of God's strength to face each day. She was able to see new opportunities and embrace the new beginning God had in store. Before long, she noticed a change in her mental attitude, in how she approached life. She had the emotional strength to invest in her children again and started speaking words of faith and hope over their lives. Eventually, she received her nursing certification, and today she is the head nurse at a well-known nonprofit clinic. Her children are now grown and successful as well. It all started when she made the choice to release her balloons and not allow the discouragement and offenses to weigh her down and keep her from her destiny.

Why don't you release *your* balloons today? Let go of all offenses and give them to God. You can accomplish so much more when you allow forgiveness to fill your heart. It is then that the door to your heart is open and you make room for God to release His healing in your life.

Forgiveness doesn't mean that what the other person did was right or excusable. It doesn't mean that the incident didn't matter. It simply means that you are trusting God and allowing Him to move you past your hurts and pain and into your divine destiny.

Some people think they can't forgive, because it seems too difficult. But in reality, it's more difficult for us when we choose *not* to forgive. Our bitterness is not hurting the person who offended us. It is only embedding itself in our heart and keeping us from God's best.

I've heard it said that forgiveness is setting the prisoner free and then realizing the prisoner was you. Choose freedom by choosing forgiveness! We spend so much time worrying and fretting over what other people think about us, but usually they aren't thinking about us at all. We need to learn not to be so touchy. Don't waste precious time wondering, *Now, what did he mean by that? Why did she say that? What was that look about?* Before you know it, you have made a big issue out of nothing.

It's important to recognize that forgiveness is more than mere words; it's a heart attitude that induces a spiritual transformation.

In 1981, my mother-in-law, Dodie Osteen, was diagnosed with terminal cancer of the liver and was told she had only a few weeks to live. No medical treatments for the disease were available to her at that time, and the doctors said there was nothing they could do for her. She and her husband, John, went home after they heard the report, got on their knees, and asked God for a miracle. Over the next year, Dodie did everything she knew to be in a position to receive her miracle. It took about a year of standing and fighting through all the symptoms, but she did receive her miracle healing! Whenever she shares her story, she talks about how one of the main keys to receiving God's healing was her willingness to let go of offenses, keeping her heart clean through the power of forgiveness. She tells how she wrote letters of forgiveness to people — her husband, her children, her parents, or anyone she could think of whom she might have offended or who might have offended her. She went the extra mile to make sure her heart was free of any offenses that would have blocked God's healing in her life.

That's the power of forgiveness. Sometimes we don't necessarily *feel* like forgiving, but when we humbly obey God in this area, He will work a miracle in our lives. There may be times in your life that you have to ask God to help you release offenses that create unforgiveness in your heart.

I encourage you today, if someone has wronged you and you still get that cringing feeling on the inside when you see that person or think about him, take it to God and allow Him to keep your heart soft and sensitive. Remember, no one's offending words or deeds define who you are or affect your intrinsic value.

Realize today, even though life is not always fair, God is always fair. He is a God of justice and He is the one who is working with you to make a beautiful pearl in the midst of your difficulties. It's okay to say, "God, I don't feel like I can forgive this person, but I'm asking You to give me the grace and the strength to help me forgive. I am giving my heart to You, and I am giving that person and situation to You, because You are the only One who can help me forgive." If we are going to change any part of our lives, we have to start on the inside. Change always begins in the heart.

To experience a true attitude change, we have to see our difficulties differently. If you have been mistreated or disrespected, or have gone through a setback in your marriage or on your job, don't let that become the major focal point of your life. Don't let that be all that you can see. Instead, get up every morning and say, "God, You are in control of my life, and even though this is difficult, even though it's not fair, I know You are going to bring me out to a better place." It is up to us to push out the circumstances and irritants that would try to attach themselves to us and weigh us down.

It may not be your fault; you may have had unfair things happen, maybe you had a difficult upbringing. God sees every person who has hurt you and every unfair situation that has happened to you. But remember, it's not what happened *to* you but what's happening *in* you that matters the most. Why don't you release the balloons? Let go of any offense. Trust God to take those pains and turn them into priceless pearls. Pearls of wisdom, pearls of strength, pearls of joy. As you let go of your balloons, you'll be free to accomplish your goals, free to enjoy your relationships, free to love your life in a fresh new way.

ANCHOR THOUGHTS

I will give God the things that irritate me: my frustrations, obstacles, and worries, knowing that as I release those irritants, He will turn them into priceless pearls.

I believe I am made in the image of God. I have the right gifts, personality, and ability to fulfill my purpose.

I will correct the small issues in my life. I will not allow any disrespect, unkindness, or negative attitudes to grow in my heart and rob me from the fruitful life God has in store.

I will forgive the people who have wronged me, releasing any bitterness or offense, trusting God to move me past those hurts and pains into a new season for my life.

8
ENJOYING RICH RELATIONSHIPS

A couple of years ago, I was chatting with a young man who had come to one of Joel's book signings. He told me that Joel's book had really helped him to recover from a terrible divorce. He didn't understand what had gone wrong in his five-year marriage. "After all," he said, "we met through a very reputable matchmaker website." He then said, "I guess I am living proof that those sites don't really work." He went on to tell me that he had filled out the profile and that his computer-matched wife had every quality he desired in a woman and he had every quality she desired in a man. I imagined him filling out the profile much like one might custom-order a car. He wanted a blond woman who loved the outdoors and quiet walks on the beach. Perhaps he also ordered a woman who liked to keep a clean house, was a good cook, and wanted exactly 3.5 children — two boys and one and a half girls! He even told me that he had specifically requested that she be of a certain Christian denomination (Presbyterian, I think). Apparently the problems began during the second year of their marriage when he realized that she didn't really meet all of his standards. He still wasn't sure if she lied on the profile, changed after they got married, or whether the profile itself was flawed. He actually said to me, "They never asked, 'Are you willing to be there when your husband needs you?' "

My encounter with this young man confirmed a universal truth regarding all types of relationships: We enter into relationships with set standards and expectations. When people do not meet the standards we set, we become disenchanted with the relationship, allowing disappointment and frustration to set in. It's easy to get along with people when everything is going great, when others are meeting our standards and acting exactly the way we want them to. But what happens when something goes wrong and our feelings get hurt or that person says something he or she shouldn't have said? Maybe your husband doesn't give you that verbal affirmation that you yearn for, or you have a friend who's always running late even though he knows how punctual you are. If you're not careful, you'll begin to focus on the unmet expectations and the disappointments, allowing them to affect your attitude, and ultimately your relationship.

But it doesn't have to be that way, if we will learn to have realistic expectations and let people off the hook. By giving people room to be human, we can avoid a lot of heartache. Accept the fact that nobody is perfect and even the best people will fail us at times. We can't hold mistakes and failures against the people in our lives when they disappoint us. It is not up to anyone in our lives to keep us happy and content. That is our own responsibility. Too often, we expect our mate to cheer us up when we are down and to always be loving and kind. We expect our boss to recognize our hard work, and our friends to always be there for us. But those are unrealistic expectations. The perfect spouse does not exist; neither does the perfect boss or the perfect friend. We would avoid a lot of disappointments by simply understanding that no matter how much you love people, no matter how much they love you, at some point, they won't live up to your expectations or they will hurt your feelings in some way. Oftentimes the people who are closest to you do not realize they have hurt you; they may not always be sensitive to your needs. That's why you have to depend on your God-given inner strength as your source of fulfillment. You can't expect anyone else to heal your hurts or meet your deepest needs. God alone can heal us and meet our needs through His perfect love.

When Jonathan was a little boy, we bought him a hamster that he affectionately named Hammy. He was so excited. Jonathan loved that little furry guy, and he enjoyed having his cousins over to play with his new friend. Occasionally, he would even let his little sister hold Hammy.

One day Jonathan reached into the cage just as always, and evidently that little hamster didn't want to be bothered, because he bit Jonathan. Jonathan was shocked. He immediately pulled his hand back and kept his distance. You could see the disappointment on Jonathan's face. Every time he looked at that hamster, he thought about it biting him. He began to tell his little sister, "Watch out; that hamster might bite you, too. I wouldn't touch him if I were you." Jonathan focused on that hamster bite so much that before long he forgot all about the fun he previously had with Hammy. He no longer loved that hamster; in fact he didn't like him at all! We ended up giving

Hammy to some of our cousins.

How many times have we seen this same situation play out in our own relationships? Someone comes into your life and you really love that person. You have so much fun spending time with your new friend, but then the friend does something to disappoint you. Your friend doesn't meet your expectations, and you begin dwelling on the negative aspects of that person. Before long, you've identified every flaw in your friend and decided that person isn't worth your investment of time and energy. Or you have a friend or a family member who you've loved for a long time, but one day that person hurts you much like Jonathan's hamster hurt him, and you simply can't get over it. Every time you look at that person, you relive that hurt all over again and you build barriers around your heart where that person is concerned.

The Scripture says, *Love keeps no record of wrongs.*[16] If we are not careful, we will start compiling a mental record of all the times someone hurts us. Every time that person makes a mistake or disappoints us, we add it to the list. Maybe the same problem comes up repeatedly and the next time it happens, you have an automatic recording in your mind that plays, "Here he goes again." The next thing you know, you are verbally reciting the list of wrongs, or silently rehearsing it in your mind until you are completely frustrated and unhappy.

You have to be willing to delete the list from your mental files. The only way to do this is through forgiveness. Just as God promises to forgive us, He wants us to forgive one another. We have to clean the slate often and make the decision that no matter what someone does to us, we are not going to hold on to the offense and allow it to pollute our lives. I am not saying you should be a doormat or let people walk all over you. But you can't measure others by using unrealistic expectations and expect a good relationship.

At every Lakewood service, we have prayer time. During this portion of the service, members and visitors pray one on one with one of the five hundred volunteers who serve as prayer partners. Both Joel and I are prayer partners, and each of us will pray for two or three people during each service. I remember one particular Saturday-night service when a fifty-something woman came up to me and asked that I pray for her marriage. She told me that her husband had always been hard to live with, but he had become even more so lately. She recited two or three of his most current offenses, and then to my surprise, she handed me three sheets of notebook paper.

She said, "Read this. It is a list of the things he has done, just in the last two weeks."

I opened the pages to see one offense after the other scribbled in various colors of ink and pencil. "He's done all this in just two weeks?" I asked.

"Yes," she said. "I didn't think anyone would believe me so I have been writing them down."

"Why so many colors of ink?" I asked.

"Well," she said, "I write them down as quickly as I can so I won't forget them, and I grab the first pen or pencil I can find. If I wait too long, I'll forget."

After I prayed for her, I thought, *Wouldn't her life be so much better if she did forget?* Any time someone disappoints you or does not meet your expectations, you have a choice to either dwell on those disappointments or overlook them. However, if you *really* want to succeed in your relationship, there is a third choice: Ignore the other person's shortcomings and immediately find something in him or her that exceeds your expectations. Most of the time, you will find dozens of good qualities in that person and only a few things that irritate you. When those irritations come up, you must remind yourself of all the good things that person brings to your life and focus on the benefits of being in a healthy relationship.

After I prayed for the woman with the list of grievances against her husband, an interesting thing happened. Following the service, Richard, another prayer partner in our ministry, approached me and asked, "Did I see you pray for a woman today with a list of things her husband has done wrong?"

"Yes," I said. "Do you know her?"

"I prayed for her Wednesday night," he responded. "She showed me the same list. It has inspired me to keep a list concerning Lisa."

I was surprised to hear Richard say this, as I knew him and his wife Lisa pretty well and had always thought they had a good relationship. For a moment I was unsure exactly how to respond. "Oh," I said, searching for the right thing to say. "Surely Lisa doesn't do that much wrong."

"No, she really doesn't," he said. "But when she does, I am going to begin keeping a different list. My list is going to have all of the things I love about her. I am going to write down all of my favorite dishes that she prepares for dinner and all the other things she does for me that make my life easier. I am going to keep the list in a drawer." He went on: "I am going to write them down as soon as I think of them, and I'm going to use the first pen I can find."

"So you won't forget them?" I asked.

"So I won't forget them," he answered.

I loved Richard's approach, and I especially loved that he drew such a good lesson from what was such a sad situation. You have to train yourself to focus on the benefits of the relationship rather than its shortcomings.

When I was sixteen years old and my friends and I were first beginning to drive, I had a friend who thought it was so funny to pull into the hamburger drive-through and order steaks and lobster. It was really rather silly, since she couldn't see the expressions on the order taker's face, but she loved to do it anyway.

Part of having realistic expectations in a relationship is to understand what you can and cannot expect from other people. No matter how much you may be craving surf and turf, don't expect to get it from the Mc-Donald's drive-through. They just don't have it. In the same way, you can't expect some things from people emotionally if they don't have it to give.

Perhaps some people never received the affirmation and support they needed, and as a result, they don't know how to give it. If your spouse was never encouraged growing up, he may not know how to encourage you today. If your husband doesn't talk a lot or show affection the way you want him to, understand that he may not know how. *You can't expect him to give you what he doesn't have to give.* Sure, he can change over time, but he may never be as good at expressing his love as you would like him to be.

However, not all is lost; you do have influence. If you're looking for something different in your relationships today, you might need to look at yourself. Most times, when you see something missing in your relationship, it's because you are the one who brings that attribute to the relationship. *You* carry the seeds of change. If you want more encouragement in your home, be the encourager. If you want more affection and tenderness in your home, show your affection to the people in your home. *Relationships are just as much about what you give as what you are hoping to receive.*

When it came to showing affection, no two people were more different than my mother and my father — at least in the beginning of their relationship. My father grew up in a home where his parents did not openly demonstrate their affection. They loved each other very much, but each just expected the other to know it. Their philosophy was that you can love someone, but you didn't have to constantly say it. When we would visit, there were hugs when we arrived and when we departed, but there were few in between. They were wonderful and loving people, but it was not natural for them to openly display their affection.

My mother grew up quite differently. She grew up in a very affectionate Southern family where you would hug someone before you left for the grocery store. (After all, you weren't going to see them for at least thirty minutes!) When I think back on all of those Christmas holidays and summer vacations we spent with my mother's family, it is the atmosphere of warmth and affection that I remember most.

As a result, my mother was the one who brought that atmosphere of warmth and affection into our home. She was always expressive with her love — constantly kissing and tenderly hugging us. Not a single day went by without her saying that she loved us. We always knew how much we meant to her because she told us so, all the time.

I realize now that my mother's persistent displays of affection profoundly changed my father. Quite simply, she showed him so much affection that he eventually lowered his guard and began to return the affection — not only with her, but with my brother and me as well. I'm sure it didn't happen overnight, but once it did, my father was changed forever. Because of his upbringing, I am sure that displays of affection do not come as naturally to my father as my mother; however, I would never have known that growing up with him. He never hesitated to show that he loved me, and even today he is warm and affectionate toward me, Joel, and his grandchildren. In fact, he still kisses my brother Don on the cheek!

You have so much to contribute to your relationships. Give your spouse and the people in your life something to draw from. *You* can be the model of change. Don't push people to change; instead, lead by example and by sowing good seeds. Simply, *be* the change you want to see.

Being a model of change doesn't mean approaching relationships with an I'm-going-to-fix-you attitude. Sometimes it is easy for us to think we are on this earth to give everyone some wisdom and help straighten him or her out, but we're not. Most people already know the areas they need to work on. They don't need you to point out their shortcomings. When we start "fixing" everyone around us, we miss the true riches we were meant to gain from those relationships. When you set out to "fix" someone, what you're really saying is, "You're not good enough the way you are, so I am going to fix you!" But that's not what people need. People need to know they are loved unconditionally. They need to know that we approve of them — even when they miss the mark on occasion. They want to know they can count on our love and support no matter what happens. If you find that you are correcting or teaching someone in every conversation, you probably need to adjust your approach with people.

I have to admit, I fell into this habit with my own children. It was not that I thought there was anything wrong with them; I just recognized that as a parent there is so little time to impart wisdom into their lives before they are living on their own. I wanted to pour into them as much as possible. I found myself using every moment as a teaching opportunity.

One day I realized that my approach was

out of balance. I still believe it is important to instill wisdom and impart good values to my children, but I believe that it is just as important to listen to them, learn from them, and enjoy them as the people God made them to be. So now I still teach them and impart my wisdom into them; I just don't spend every waking moment doing it. In addition, I have grown to accept that they will learn some of life's lessons on their own.

To make the most of our relationships with others, we have to balance our expectations of them with the grace of allowing them to be who they are. You may think you have the perfect solution to someone else's inadequacies; and because you want only the best for them, you feel justified in telling them so. However, don't fall into the trap of feeling you need to get your point across or teach a life lesson in every conversation. Don't try to fix them. Instead, just relax and enjoy your relationship.

Katherine was in her late twenties when her younger sister, who was fresh out of college, came to live with her. Katherine made some mistakes early in her life and wanted to make sure her younger sister didn't follow the same path. She wanted to help equip her for life as best she could, so she was constantly trying to show her the right way to go. The two had a great relationship, but the younger sister started feeling like she had a second mother! She felt like she couldn't do anything right because the older sister was constantly showing her a better way.

One day Katherine came home to find her younger sister in tears, sitting on the bed next to her packed suitcase.

"What's wrong?" asked Katherine.

Her sister looked at her, and through her sobs said, "I feel so broken. My whole life is one big mistake!"

At that moment Katherine realized that she had been too hard on her sister. "You're not broken," she said. "I am."

Years later, they were able to laugh about it, because ironically, the younger sister caught herself approaching her own daughter in the same way.

The truth is we have all been guilty of trying to fix those around us. In fact my mother used to say, "If I could open up your head and pour my knowledge into it, I would." But she couldn't, and neither can I . . . and neither can you!

We have to give others the grace to learn on their own. No one wants to hear "I told you so," or be reminded that "You could have done it better if only you had listened to me." Give people the grace to learn in their own way. Balance grace and truth and allow others to make their own choices, even if they're not what you would have chosen. Remember, love covers all; and in relationships, love and acceptance are what build the bridges between our hearts.

God desires for you to have deep, lasting relationships built on mutual understanding and having realistic expectations of each other.

A good relationship is really just a decision. Whether your boss refuses to affirm you or your close friend didn't include you in a social outing — even if your sister forgot to call you on your birthday — you must make a choice to simply adjust your view of that person and what you expect from him or her.

Every day we have the opportunity to prove our compassion. Either we can go around angry, holding a grudge, or we can let go of offenses and put ourselves in the other person's shoes and be more understanding.

I once read a story about a woman who was going through a very difficult time in her life. Her mother, with whom she was extremely close, passed away from a sudden heart attack. She was devastated by her mother's death, and the pain was so over-whelming that she didn't think she could get over it. During her grieving period, she would force herself to get up in the morning to get her young son ready for school and make her husband breakfast before he went to work. Many close friends sent beautiful flowers, wrote meaningful condolence cards, and reached out with a loving hand to the family. She knew she needed to write thank-you cards to all the people who had shown such kindness and compassion to her, and eventually, she got to the point where she was strong enough to do that.

It took her several days, but every morning after getting her son and husband out the door, she sat at the dining room table and wrote the notes, pouring her heart out to the people who had been there for her during this difficult time. Writing those notes became a time of healing for her as she reflected on her life. After four or five days, she finished the notes, gave them to her husband, and said, "If you will mail these for me tomorrow at the office, I can now start living my life without my mother." He took the letters and said, "Of course I will."

One morning a few weeks later she saw her husband's tennis bag lying on the floor.

Her husband always played tennis after he left the office, and she thought, *I need to start preparing his tennis bag as I have always done before.* So she picked up the bag and tossed it onto the bed to get it ready for the next day. She noticed a big bulge in the side of the bag and figured her husband probably left some old sweaty T-shirts in the side pocket. As she reached into the bag, to her surprise, it wasn't a dirty T-shirt, it was the bag of thank-you notes she had written — her husband had never mailed them. Standing there looking at the bag, she felt her heart break into a million pieces. She thought, *How could this matter so little to him? If he loves me, why didn't he remember to do something that was so important to me?* As she stood there sobbing, her husband walked into the room and saw the bag of notes in her hand. With a look of shock on his face, he said, "Oh my . . . I forgot to mail them." He instantly began apologizing and telling her that he would do whatever it took to make it up to her. He would take the day off and hand-deliver all the notes himself. He knew he had made a mistake and was extremely sorry for it.

She was devastated — shocked, sad, and angry all at the same time. She felt that she had every right to rant and rave, to make him feel as horrible as she felt. After all, this was so important to her. Nevertheless, somehow she managed to look into his face, and with an accepting heart, she made the choice to forgive. *After all,* she thought, *what would it really benefit their relationship to punish him in her time of anger and hurt? What would it gain in the long run to make him suffer even more for his mistake?*

At that moment, her husband saw her for who she really was — a compassionate, forgiving women who loved him no matter what, and who would forgive unconditionally.

We must understand that our disappointments are for a season, but our relationships are for a lifetime.

CHOOSE LOVE

We all have a choice in how we deal with our anger and how we respond to the people who have hurt and disappointed us. The woman in the story had the wisdom to understand that this season in her life was temporary, but that her relationship with her husband would last a lifetime. She chose to focus on the long-term aspects of her relationship rather than the short-term gratification she may have felt by responding in anger.

Our relationships are precious, valuable treasures from heaven, and we should handle them carefully, always looking for ways to build bridges to each other's hearts. It is so important that we choose to focus on the long-term effects of our decisions instead of the gratification of the moment.

She understood the power of her words and the lasting effect they could have on her husband and their relationship. She chose love.

I often hear people say that it is actions, not words, that matter. I think both matter, especially when you consider that God spoke the universe into existence with His words. In the same way, we can create or destroy with ours. It is important to understand that our words, while only puffs of sound, can have a deep and permanent effect. When we choose our words, we choose strife or we choose love. It is that simple.

There is a story about a little boy who had a bad temper. His father gave him a bag of nails and told him that every time he lost his temper and lashed out with his words, he would have to hammer a nail into their beautiful white picket fence. The first day after the father made this deal with his son, the young boy drove eight nails into the fence. Over the next few weeks, however, as the boy learned to control his anger, the number of nails he had to hammer each day drastically decreased. Finally the day came when the boy didn't lose his temper at all. He was so proud of himself, so he told his father about his accomplishment. The father put his arm around his son, walked him out to the fence, and told the boy to remove a nail for each day that he didn't lose his temper. Quite a while passed when finally the young boy was able to remove that last nail. As soon as he finished, the boy ran to tell his father.

The dad hugged the little boy and said, "You have done so well at keeping your temper in check, and I'm proud of you, but I want you to see something."

The father took the young boy by the hand and walked over to the fence.

"See all these holes in our beautiful fence?" the father asked.

The little boy nodded his head.

"That fence will never be the same," the father said. "When you say things in anger, those words leave scars just like the nail holes in our fence. You can pull the nails out, but the marks are deep and they are permanent. The same goes for our words. It won't matter how many times you say you're sorry, you can't take those words back, and the scars are still there."

The boy's eyes filled with tears as he looked at the beautiful fence, now riddled with holes.

"Please forgive me, Daddy, for the holes I put in you."

The father smiled at his son and gave him a big hug. "Of course I do, son," he said. "Of course I do. But, from now on, let's think before we speak, and always speak so our words won't hurt someone else."

Joel and I were young when we married, and like most young married couples, we had to make some big adjustments. Although we were head over heels in love, quite simply, we were learning to live together. Sometimes irritations would creep in — some small, some large — and before long those irritations began affecting the way I communicated with my husband. Sometimes I chose words that were insensitive or unkind.

Several months into our marriage, Joel and I had a disagreement, and instead of letting it go and just agreeing to disagree, I said something that I knew I shouldn't have. I could see those words really hurt him. He no longer wanted to finish the conversation; he simply left the room. As I sat there, I pondered what had just happened.

It was then that I felt God speak to me deep down in my spirit. Even as I am writing these words, they are as real to me today as they were the day He spoke them into my heart. He said, "Victoria, if you don't change your words, you're going to change the man you married. Your words are going to cause him to build a wall around his heart and that will change the foundation of your relationship."

Those words instantly pierced my heart and tears began to well in my eyes. I was crushed at the thought of destroying my relationship with my husband. I dearly loved him; I loved his gentle spirit, and I didn't want him to change. At that moment, I chose to love Joel exactly the way he was.

Somehow I had slipped into focusing on the wrong things, little things that were not even significant, yet I allowed them to upset me to such a degree that it threatened the beautiful relationship we had. Right then I made the decision to start overlooking those little irritations and to begin focusing on unconditional love and acceptance in our relationship. Instead of getting upset, I took the time to understand my husband and to see his side of things. I chose to magnify the good qualities in him.

As I began overlooking those little irritations, Joel responded the same way. The more I treat Joel like a king, the more he treats me like his queen. The more I focus on the good in him, the more he focuses on the good in me.

We have grown together. We have learned together, and, as far as I am concerned, we have built the best relationship in the world.

I learned an important lesson that day; that we must handle our relationships with great care and that love doesn't just happen — we must choose it.

KEEPING THE CONNECTIONS

Novelist Katherine Anne Porter once wrote, "Love must be learned, and learned again; there is no end to it." Love should not remain the same year after year; love is supposed to grow. Relationships evolve over time, people change over time, and our love should strengthen and grow over time, too. The Apostle Paul prayed that our love would abound and grow in knowledge and depth of insight. That tells me that I cannot put my love on autopilot. If we put our love on autopilot and trust that the people in our lives will simply know that we love them, our relationships will not grow or will not be as fruitful as they were intended to be. That's why it's so important to make every effort to keep strong connections in our relationships.

Several years ago when Joel and I assumed leadership at the ministry, our lives became fuller and more complicated. We had to make an extra effort to connect with each other throughout the day. Oftentimes we found ourselves moving in different directions, so we looked for ways to keep a strong connection. If we weren't careful, we could find ourselves breezing right by each other, our minds preoccupied with the tasks at hand. Instead, we chose to acknowledge each other — to make a connection — each time we passed. Sometimes we high-five, sometimes it's a quick "I love you"; occasionally he'll plant a kiss right on my lips. It's not important how we connect, but that we *do* connect. We are both busy people. We both have a lot going on, but whenever we see each other, everything else is placed on hold for a moment while we connect. When we take time to keep our connections strong, it helps keep our hearts moving in the same direction.

This is just as important with our children. When they were younger, I would sit on their beds with them at night and read them bedtime stories. Now that they are older, they don't want that anymore, so I've found other ways to keep the connections. I make sure they know my heart is open toward them, and I do what I can to create an atmosphere of love and security in our home. Sometimes just a simple smile as we walk by each other is a way to say "You're important to me." Sometimes when I walk by their rooms, I poke my head inside for a moment and say "I love you," then close the door. I also do little things like putting notes in their lunchboxes that say "You're the greatest. I think you're so special."

Leaving notes is a wonderful and easy way to keep connections. When Joel travels without me, I put little notes in his socks just to say "I love you." I have also been known to put photos of us in his suitcase. You may want to leave sweet notes around the house, in a drawer, under a pillow, or on the television remote control as little reminders to the people you love that they are valuable to you.

Recreational activities are another way we keep the connections in our family. It used to be a challenge figuring out what we wanted to do as a family. Now we have a jar in the kitchen and every time someone has an idea for a family activity, we write it down and put it in the jar. Then when we have time together, we pull an idea out of the jar. It makes it fun and interesting for our children . . . and for Joel and me as well.

I encourage you to take time with your family. Eat meals together. Have a date night with your husband. Joel and I reserve every Friday night just for us. We may not go out every Friday night, but we always spend it together and without distractions.

We realize how important it is to get out of the same old rut. We have to keep it fresh. Sometimes we like to surprise each other on our date nights. One time I took Joel out, but I would not tell him where we were going. He kept asking all sorts of questions. "What do I wear? How long will it take to get there?" To his surprise, I took him to a local amusement park. We had the best time! He could not wait to go back.

Do something spontaneous with your spouse; ride go-carts or have a picnic in the park. Do the things you used to do when you were dating. Keep the connections with your words, with your heart, and with your actions.

You can connect with anyone with whom you have a relationship. Not long ago, Joel preached a message on the power of encouraging words. He told the story of how a teacher encouraged each person in the class to make a list of the positive things he or she saw in the other students. Years later, one of the students joined the military and was killed in the line of duty. When they recovered his body and looked inside his wallet, they found several lists neatly tucked inside. For more than five years, he had cherished those wonderful sentiments his classmates wrote about him.

The next week after Joel taught that message, as I was preparing for a family trip, I noticed two envelopes on my desk, one addressed to me, the other addressed to Joel. When I opened mine, I saw that it was a note from Joel's sister, Lisa. Her note read: "What's in your wallet? I just wanted to tell you what I see in you." She wrote the most wonderful things to me, and like that young soldier did, I will always cherish them. Those words meant so much to me. I was touched that Lisa took the time to put into practice the teaching that she received.

It takes time and effort to maintain the connections in our relationships. When someone offends us we can be tempted to disconnect. One of the most common mistakes we make is to give someone the silent treatment as a means by which to disconnect.

I heard a story about a couple who had a

big fight. That night the man and wife were still not talking to each other, and since the man didn't want to give in first, he left her a note saying, "Wake me up at six o'clock in the morning." The next morning, the man woke up at eight o'clock and was furious. He was about to go find his wife and give her a piece of his mind when he noticed a note on his side of the bed that read, "It's six o'clock; wake up!"

At one time or another, we have all faced the temptation to disconnect by giving someone the silent treatment. After being married to Joel for more than twenty-one years, I have learned that is not the best way to handle a disagreement.

The Scripture encourages, "Don't let the sun go down on your anger." It's not good to go to sleep mad and frustrated, because you'll wake up with that same anger and frustration you went to bed with — and you probably won't sleep very well anyway. You may not have the resolution to the disagreement by the time the evening comes, but if you will learn that you can disagree and still be friends, you will enjoy your relationships a whole lot more.

I have a friend who tells me that sometimes when she and her husband are still mad at each other at bedtime, right before she goes to sleep, she will simply say to him, "I am right, you are wrong, and I love you. Good night."

I mentioned in an earlier chapter that Joel and I have decided that it's okay to agree to disagree. One of the most freeing experiences for a couple is to recognize that they are two different people who see things differently and who can still love each other and stay connected. Just because you have a disagreement with your friends or family members does not mean there are not plenty of other areas on which you see eye to eye. It just means you have a difference of opinion. Having the same heart and the same goal is what maintains a good connection. There will be times we do not always agree on every decision or subject, but we should always believe in each other, support each other, and move forward through life together — connected.

First Corinthians, Chapter 13, says that love bears all things and that love believes the best about a person.[17] That means when your spouse is a little short with you or hurts your feelings, you don't react with harsh words or pout. Instead, you say to yourself, "He must be having a hard day, because that's not like him." This principle works with every person in your life. Choose to see the best in your children and stay connected to them even when they act unlovable. Choose to go the extra mile with your coworker, even if she doesn't return the favor. Choose to magnify the good in others and overlook the bad. Stay connected and watch how your relationships will improve.

If we are going to create a heaven-on-earth atmosphere in our homes or a peaceful environment in the workplace, or have strong relationships with our friends, we must choose to stay connected on a daily basis.

I like the way former First Lady Abigail Adams once explained it. She said that true love is not based on spending every waking moment gazing into each other's eyes, but rather casting our gaze in the same direction. When we maintain strong connections and share the love that God has placed inside each one of us, we'll enjoy the richness that our relationships were meant to bring. Let me encourage you to do your part to keep the connections. Be quick to forgive, don't keep score, but do have realistic expectations. Remember, the disappointments are only for a season, but our relationships are for a lifetime. As you allow others the freedom to be who God made them to be, you'll enjoy your relationships more and your journey together will be happy, healthy, and whole.

ANCHOR THOUGHTS

I will have realistic expectations regarding those with whom I am in a relationship. I will choose to see the best, give them the grace to make mistakes and the freedom not to be perfect.

I will make every effort to keep strong connections in my relationships. I will not put my love on autopilot. I will take time for those I love. I will bless them with my words. I will express my feelings with hugs, kisses, and smiles.

I realize it's not up to any other person to keep me happy and content. I will take responsibility for my own happiness and depend on my God-given inner strength for my source of fulfillment.

I will not keep an account of the wrongs done to me. I will keep an account of the things I admire and love about the people in my life. I'll not be easily offended and go to sleep holding on to anger and frustration. I will start each day with a fresh new attitude. I realize my relationships are just as much about what I give as what I receive.

I acknowledge that my relationships are for a lifetime. When others disappoint me and don't meet my expectations, I will choose my words carefully. I will be full of mercy and build bridges to the hearts of those I love.

I recognize that I can't make people change. I can't force someone to be a certain way. I can only be a model for change. When I treat people the way I want them to be, that's the seed God uses to bring about change.

9
DISCOVERING WHAT
OTHERS NEED

Sometimes minor adjustments in your approach to people can make a major difference in the quality of your relationships. And your relationships have a direct impact on the quality of your life. You can have all the money in the world, a great job, and wonderful opportunities in front of you, but if you don't have good relationships, you're not going to enjoy your life the way God intended. One of the keys to making the most of your relationships is learning to study and adapt to the people in your life. I have been studying Joel for a long time. In fact, I can remember studying him as early as our second date.

Joel came over to my house for dinner — and no, that wasn't the last time I cooked for him! We were talking in the kitchen as I was putting the finishing touches on the salad. I started asking him question after question about various scriptures in the

Bible because, after all, he was John Osteen's son, and I thought he'd want to talk about spiritual things. Surprisingly, he didn't seem too interested. At one point in the conversation, I asked him about a specific scripture and said, "You probably know where that is found," and handed him a Bible. Joel began flipping through the pages, but before long, he put the Bible down without even answering my Bible trivia question.

I was stunned! I said, "I can't believe you don't know where that is found! I thought you'd be a spiritual giant."

Joel said nothing and just grinned at me as we carried on with the evening.

I found out later, the day after our dinner, he jokingly told all his friends that I had called him a spiritual midget. Of course that wasn't exactly true, but that's the way he likes to remember it.

But how I remember it is that Joel was not out to impress me with fancy words and lofty knowledge. I later realized Joel had read his Bible every day since he was a little boy and knew more about Scripture than I ever imagined. It's not always what a person says, but what he does and how he does it that communicates the most about his character. As we began dating, I took every opportunity to study how Joel treated his family and how he talked about his friends and the people in his life. I observed how disciplined he was and how he was always on time everywhere he went. I noticed how he would always lend a generous hand to the people around him. I took note of the people he surrounded himself with and the things he enjoyed doing. I paid special attention to how he treated me and talked to me, and he was always consistent in his actions. His example meant more to me than if he would have been able to quote a whole book from the Bible.

It's important to really study and know the people you allow into your life. Actions speak louder than words. If you are single today, take the time to watch a person's life before you give him your heart. If you are considering a business deal, take time to learn the character of the person you are dealing with before you make a commitment. Don't ignore the red flags. When questionable character issues show up repeatedly, pay attention. Ask yourself, "Could this be telling me something I need to know in the future?"

The key to loving relationships is to know well the people you allow into your close circle. When you know and understand the people with whom you are in a relationship, you can better adapt to them in the future. Even before Joel asked me to marry him, I knew he was the *kind of person* I wanted to marry. I studied everything I could about him during the year and a half we dated. I did my research, and as much as is humanly possible, I felt certain I could live with what I knew about him for the rest of my life.

Don't go into a marriage relationship thinking, *As soon as we tie the knot, then I can change the person I am marrying.* I remember my father always saying to me, "Victoria, if you don't like something about the person you are going to marry, don't think you can change him when you get married; it will probably only get worse." Don't go into a serious relationship thinking you have the power to change that person, because it is unrealistic and not fair to that person.

Someone asked me one time if Joel was perfect. "Yes, he is perfect for me," I answered. Marriage is a commitment even when circumstances are not always perfect. However, if you are willing to study and learn about the people in your life, you can make minor adjustments that can make a major difference.

After more than twenty-one years of marriage, I am still studying and adapting to Joel, as he does to me, and it has made a huge difference in the quality of our marriage. As long as you live, things are going to change in your life, and you have to be willing to be flexible and change with them. If your spouse gets a job that takes him out of town more often, then you may need to make some adjustments. Maybe your best friend had a new baby and she can't meet you regularly for lunch like she did before the birth of her child. Have you noticed your boss took on more responsibility and needs a little extra help on Monday mornings? If we will be flexible and willing to change, we will have greater relationships and enjoy our lives more.

I encourage you to study the people in your life: your friends, your boss, your spouse, your children. Notice their likes and dislikes. Notice what frustrates them and observe what makes them happy. What do they need, or to what do they best respond? When some people are stressed out, they need encouragement; others need space. Some people need compliments and affirmation, while others simply need a little time. There's no one-size-fits-all way to relate to the people in your life. If you're going to get more out of your relationships, you have to study others and find out what they need — and then do your best to provide it. We should have the attitude that says, "What can I do to get along better with the people in my life?" not "How can I change my boss?" or "How can I get my husband to treat me better?"

Turn it around and ask yourself, "What can I do?" If you will help other people with their needs, God will use that as a seed to meet your needs.

I always chuckle to myself, because I can set my watch by Joel's routine. I know what day he studies to prepare to write his message, and I know what day he writes it. I know when he is going to break for lunch and how long he is going to take to eat it. I know when he is going to come out of his office and what he is going to do after that. He is highly disciplined and precise. In the morning I am busy getting our children ready for school, so I don't spend much time with Joel until lunch. We both work from home, so whenever I can, I will go downstairs and eat lunch with him.

A few years ago, I thought that lunchtime would be the perfect opportunity to sit down and spend some time with Joel. That was great Monday through Wednesday. Thursday, however, is the day he writes his messages, and when I would sit down to join him, I noticed he was not very talkative. He never said anything to me about it, but I could tell by his actions that he didn't really want any company. He would finish his lunch and go back to his office to continue working on the message he was preparing to present that weekend. After this happened a few times, I realized that Joel didn't enjoy talking during Thursday lunches, because he wanted to keep his mind on his message and not lose his focus.

If I had not been in the habit of studying Joel and trying to learn about what's important to him, I could have easily become offended by his lack of interest in conversation during lunch. I could have started saying things like "You never make time for me" or "You never consider my feelings." I could have allowed myself to take offense at the way he was treating me. But that wouldn't have accomplished anything, and frankly, it would not have been true. Joel is marvelously thoughtful and loving toward me, which is why he didn't want to hurt my feelings by telling me he would rather eat lunch alone on Thursdays.

Not only did I realize that he did not want company for lunch on Thursdays, but I knew there was no point in getting upset or trying to change the situation; it wasn't about what *I* needed, it was about what *he* needed. So I stopped coming down to eat with him on Thursdays and didn't make a big deal about it. Joel noticed, though, and he told me later how much he appreciated the way I showed respect for him and his time. It wasn't that big of a deal for me to give up those lunchtime talks — especially since they were usually quite short — but it was a huge deal to him. It showed Joel that I honored him and that I was willing to adapt to what he needed.

Scripture says to live considerately. You have to consider the other people in your life. Study them and make the necessary adjustments so you can have healthy relationships. For example, when your spouse comes home after a long day at work and driving in rush-hour traffic, don't just hand the kids over to him when he walks in the door and tell him you are going to the mall. Wait until he is able to relax and get settled, and then let him know you need to run some errands. Better yet, if you will let him know in advance and plan it into your schedules, it can make a huge difference for both of you.

We also need to be considerate with our children. They may not want to answer twenty questions the minute you pick them up from school. Instead, wait until they have a snack and pipe down, then ask them how their day went. If you will look for the best opportunity and wait for the right time, you will have much more success and much less tension in your relationships.

When I've had a busy day and need some time to recharge, Joel can usually sense it, so he'll take the kids out to dinner or to their cousins' house, so I can have some time to myself. He knows that I like to take a hot bubble bath or get my nails done or simply escape to the mall for a while. It's amazing what an hour at the mall will do for a woman! In all seriousness, I need time to myself occasionally; it reenergizes me.

Joel is the same way; he needs time to unwind as well, although when he wants to relax and recharge his batteries, he likes to sit in his big chair in the bedroom and watch *Wheel of Fortune.* Quite often, when he wants to get his mind off things, he plays outside with the kids or plays a game of basketball with some of the guys.

We have to be willing to give the people in our lives what *they* need, which may not necessarily be what *we* need. When I need to be refreshed, Joel doesn't tell me to go play kickball in the backyard with the kids.

He doesn't say, "That's what I do, so you should do it, too." In a similar way, when he needs to clear his mind, the last thing I would suggest is for him to go to the mall! Joel and I know how important it is to be considerate of each other's needs, so we make every effort to study and adapt to each other.

When you take the time to study the people in your life and learn their ways, you will have more opportunities to spend quality time with them. Remember those lunches with Joel? Now I have a standing lunch date with him on a day when he is free to focus his full attention on me. I gave up a little and gained a lot!

It may take time to learn and understand the needs of the people with whom you are in a relationship, but if you will make the effort and be patient, it usually ends up working out to your advantage.

Not long ago, Joel and I were visiting with some friends in California and I began sharing a funny story about something that had happened to us during our travels. One of our friends started laughing and nodding his head just as I was getting into the good part of the story, so I paused and asked, "Have you heard this story before?"

"Yes," he answered. "Three minutes ago,

when Joel told it, but please continue, because your version is much funnier. Joel didn't share half of those details with us!"

Yes, Joel and I communicate differently. It doesn't mean that one of us is better than the other; it simply means that we're wired differently, so we have to learn how to adapt to each other's communication style. Over the years, I've learned that Joel doesn't like hearing every single detail of a story, even though I do. I want to know exactly what was said, who said it, and how they said it. That's why, when I tell a story, it takes me fifteen minutes and Joel can tell that same story in two minutes. Knowing this, I try not to tell him every detail, although it's not always that easy.

One time I was enthusiastically telling Joel something that I thought was important, and just as I was getting to the good part, I noticed his eyes beginning to glaze over. I began talking faster and faster, but it didn't do any good. Finally I said, "You don't want to hear this; I can tell because you are not even paying attention to me."

It wasn't anything he said; it was how he looked. I could tell by his body language that I had lost him after the first three minutes. At first I got frustrated and thought, *I am not telling him anything any-*

more. But of course that didn't last, so I just made the adjustments in my communication with him; now I try to tell him only the most important details of the story. (You and I know he's missing the real juicy parts!) When I see his eyes glazing over, I don't get upset. It's just my clue that he is going into detail overload, so I adapt to his communication style.

Maybe you're reading this and thinking, *Victoria, why would you change yourself in order to please Joel?*

The truth is, I'm not changing who I am; I'm changing the way I communicate so I can have a better relationship with my husband. I want Joel to hear me, so I adapt to the way he listens best. It is good for me and good for him.

Another way to improve your relationships and help the people around you understand you better is by simply communicating your needs. The people in your life can't read your mind. You can't always expect them to know exactly what you want or need. You should respectfully express what you like and dislike, and kindly tell them what helps you and what bothers you. When I want to discuss something with Joel, I tell him in advance, "I don't want you to try to solve my problem. I just want you to hear me out, because that will help me to work it out." All I need is for him to lend a supportive ear. Knowing this, he does his best to listen as I get my thoughts out in the open. Because Joel has an understanding of what I need and I have an understanding of what he needs, it keeps the tension out of our relationship and we can appreciate each other.

Be sensitive to the people in your life and show them respect. A lot of the tension in our homes and the pressures in our relationships could be avoided if we would be more sensitive and understanding.

Relationships are all about learning. In marriage, we are learning to become one; in families, we are learning to get along; in business, we are learning to work together; in friendship, we are learning to make allowances for one another. Life is a learning process, and the quicker you embrace that fact, the more you'll enjoy the people around you. Start today and become a student of your relationships so you will better understand the people closest to you.

One of the best ways to learn about the people in your life is to become a good listener. We can *hear* a lot of things, but when we're really listening, we're fully engaged. When people talk to you, give them your undivided attention. Look them in the eyes and have an interest in what they are saying.

One time we were on vacation, having such a fun and enjoyable time with our children, and I said, "Isn't it great to just relax and not have to run around and do anything?"

Alexandra spoke up and said, "Yeah, it's great because when Jonathan and I say something funny, Dad doesn't give us his *courtesy laugh.*"

"Courtesy laugh? What does that mean?" I asked.

"You know . . . when he's busy and not really paying attention and we say something funny, he just says, 'Ha!' But, when he is relaxed, he always gives us a real laugh and says something funny back to us."

People can tell when you are really engaged with them and want to hear what they are saying. I believe part of being respectful and considerate is to listen attentively. When you're talking with someone, you should make every effort to give them your undivided attention. Stop what you are doing for a few minutes and give the people in your life the gift of listening.

I've found this to be especially important with children. I recognized early on that my children have a need to be heard, so I have learned to be creative when communicating with them. I give them the opportunity to share their feelings and explain their points of view. It's important that they know I value and respect what they have to say. That's so much more productive than simply saying, "The answer is no — just because I said so!"

I'm not saying that you have to justify every parenting decision or sugarcoat everything you say to your children, but you can always find a way to present your point in a positive, educational way and allow some dialogue. If you have teenagers in your house, you know how important it is for them to be heard; don't shut them down with "It's not up for discussion." Sometimes they don't even care if they get their way; they simply want you to listen to them. When you listen to your children and give them your full attention, you are building their confidence and making them feel valued and loved.

No matter what the age, everyone has a deep need to be valued and respected. This means that when people are talking to you, don't interrupt them. Let them finish their thoughts. You may already know what they're going to say, but that's okay; be considerate and let them finish anyway. If someone asks you a question and you know the answer before she finishes speaking, resist the tendency to jump in there and cut him or her off with a "Here, let me tell you what to do." Just be respectful and let him or her finish. It's not only a matter of being considerate and investing good things into the lives of others, but it is letting them know you really care.

When I run errands or go shopping, I am usually in a hurry because I have only a short time to get things done. I call it power shopping. You just get what you need and get out. One particular day, I was in a hurry to get home so I could make dinner, and I must have had three or four people stop me and talk to me or ask me to pray for them. With so many things on my mind, I had to stop and engage, giving them my full attention. It is not always easy, but it is a good seed to sow, because the closest thing to the heart of God is people. If we will learn to give our best to those who need our time and attention, God will see to it that we get His best in return.

FINDING COMMON GROUND

We all encounter difficult people from time to time. You might even have had someone come to mind at the mention of the word "difficult." Chances are, that person is in your life for a reason. And one way to overcome the negativity, keep the peace, and continue working toward a mutual goal is to find common ground. Whether it's a negative family member, a hard-to-get-along-with coworker, or an unhappy person you encounter at the grocery store, if you make the effort, you can find common ground and actually get along with most people. It may take a little practice and creativity, but the end result is worth it!

Finding common ground can involve just about anything — maybe you went to the same college or you both enjoy the same hobby. Maybe you both like animals or have a mutual friend or shop at the same shoe store or like the same foods. It might be something as simple as having the same color nail polish. The point is, when you are standing on common ground, it turns the interaction in a positive direction and will help you see eye to eye.

Sometimes finding common ground means saying nothing at all and simply smiling so you can stand on the common ground of peace. This is especially true when you're in a conversation with someone whose views you don't share. Sometimes you have to let go of your need to be heard for the sake of peace.

One time Joel and I were talking to an acquaintance we hadn't seen in a while, and the man began telling us some stories and sharing his strong opinions. As Joel and I listened to this man, I thought to myself, *I don't agree at all with what this man is saying.* The man went on and on, and I knew Joel couldn't possibly be agreeing with him either, but Joel just stood there with his trademark smile on his face, nodding and engaging with this man the best way he could. Finally it was time for us to leave and Joel and I wished him well.

After we walked away, I said, "Joel, I don't know why you didn't give him your opinion. I know you don't agree with him."

Joel said something to me I will never forget. He simply said, "Victoria, *I wasn't put on this earth to straighten everyone out.*"

I knew he was right. If you feel like you have to give your opinion every time you disagree with someone, you'll waste valuable time and energy that could be used in more productive ways.

That day I received wisdom that will be with me forever — it's not my job to straighten everyone out. We need to learn that other people have a right to their opinions. We don't have to say everything that we think all the time. We don't have to be right or always prove our point. Of course, there may be times when it's appropriate to share your views and wisdom with someone, but that's very different from constantly sharing your opinions.

It works the same way in our family relationships. Recently, I had a reporter ask me if Joel and I ever argue, and I answered, "Of course we disagree, but you can't argue with someone who won't argue with you, and Joel simply won't argue."

It's not because he can't; Joel simply made up his mind a long time ago that he is going to keep peace in our home, even when we don't agree on something. Over the years, we've discovered an important key to keeping peace and unity between us — we've learned to agree to disagree. You can't get mad at someone just because he doesn't feel the same way you do about a particular subject, even if that person happens to be your spouse! Sometimes the common ground you find is that you agree to disagree. There have been many times when Joel and I have had to stop and say, "All right, we can't see eye to eye on this, and we're not going to keep going in circles over this issue. We love each other, so we're just going to agree to disagree in this situation." That's it. End of story. End of discussion.

Along those lines, I've discovered that it's not always best to try to resolve a situation in the heat of the moment. Sometimes it's better to let things cool off and get a new perspective before discussing it any further. (Besides, I can't help it if Joel's wrong sometimes . . .)

If you'll go through life allowing other people to have their own thoughts and feelings — even if they are completely contrary to yours — you'll keep your joy and peace intact. It will improve your relationships and help you be a blessing to others. When you are kind and compassionate, and looking for common ground, you have a much better chance of influencing people's opinions and speaking into their lives. I've found that in most disagreements, at some point, one of the parties is going to change his or her view to the other's side. I know if I just wait long enough, eventually my idea will become Joel's idea, and it will come to pass. Women, you know what I'm talking about! In all seriousness, it's okay to let the solution be the other person's idea. When someone takes ownership of an idea, that person is more likely to get behind it. Remember, it's not about who's right; it's about what's right, and working together toward a common goal.

One time Ruth Graham was asked if she submitted to her husband, Billy Graham. She answered, "There's a time to submit and a time to outwit." She's my kind of woman. When we study the people in our lives and make adjustments to meet their needs, our relationships are going to be healthier and more rewarding. No matter how different your backgrounds, no matter how different your views and opinions, don't allow those difficult people in your life to frustrate you or steal your joy. When you look for common ground, you'll be surprised how it can turn around a difficult situation and even open the door to greater opportunities.

I heard a story about a young man who was hired as a server at an upscale restaurant. Even though he was starting as an assistant waiter, he was excited about his job and the opportunity to eventually become a headwaiter himself. He soon discovered that the headwaiter to whom he reported was a very difficult woman. She was the top producer and had built a loyal customer base, but there was a reason for her unusual success. It turns out she didn't have much competition — she was so sarcastic and condescending to all the other waiters that they would usually end up quitting before they had a chance to be promoted. And she was starting to use those same bullying tactics on this young man. She would intentionally mess up his orders and do whatever she could to try to get him in trouble.

The young man really needed his job, so he decided he would not allow this woman to get the best of him. He knew the easy route would have been to quit and find another job, but he chose to stay and try to win her favor. One day he overheard her talking to one of her customers about her babies. He thought to himself, *I didn't know she had children.* So he decided to wait for the best opportunity to ask her about them. When he did, he found out those babies were actually her two cats, and they meant the world to her. The young man also grew up with a cat in his home, and when he mentioned it, her face totally changed and he saw an opening into her heart. Day after day, he would ask her about her cats and listen intently as she told him all about their quirky personalities. That young man found common ground with the woman, and before long she and he had a wonderful working relationship. He even stayed at the restaurant long enough to achieve his goal of advancing to headwaiter himself! Because the young man chose to sow seeds of kindness rather than treating the woman the way she was treating him, God opened a door of opportunity, and the young man was able to eventually reap a harvest of blessing in his own life.

Sometimes we have to go that extra mile to find common ground with another person. I've discovered that if you will take the time to identify with the people you encounter throughout the day, everything will go better, and your life will become more pleasant. Maybe you run into an unhappy waiter or a rude or slow checkout clerk, and you can feel yourself starting to get upset. Right then, you have a choice to make. You can *react* to her or *respond* to her. If you react, you're allowing *her* to decide your actions and you'll probably end up doing or saying something you'll regret later. But, when you choose to respond, *you* choose your actions — you can take the high road and overlook the other person's negative attitude. So the next time you run into a difficult person, remember, try to turn around that situation by finding some common ground.

Recently I shared this same principle with

a friend and she took it to heart. She said, "I'm really going to try to apply this to my life." Well, she got the opportunity to practice this principle shortly after our conversation.

My friend was attending a conference out of town and needed a ride from the convention center to the local airport. The woman who was helping organize the conference offered to arrange a ride for my friend with someone who lived locally. The woman told her, "I've arranged a ride for you, but let me warn you — Judy is your driver."

You see, Judy was known for her snippy, opinionated personality. When the two women met outside the convention center, Judy opened with "I guess I'm your ride to the airport, even though the airport is far out of my way."

As my friend loaded her luggage into Judy's hatchback, all she could think about was, *This is going to be the longest ride of my life.* After a few minutes of Judy's complaining, my friend decided to turn the situation around and do whatever she could to communicate with Judy in a meaningful way.

Just then my friend noticed a snapshot of a curly-headed little girl on Judy's key chain and said, "What a darling little girl. I love her curls." Instantly Judy's demeanor changed. She said, "She is cute, isn't she? That's my little granddaughter. Her name is Emily."

"Emily?" my friend asked. "That's my daughter's name! We named her after my grandmother."

Judy became so excited that she almost drove the car off the highway.

"You'll never believe it, but Emily is named after me!" Judy shared. "My full name is Judith Emily."

The ride that began so uncomfortably and full of negativity turned into a fun, chatty, positive trip simply because my friend made an effort to find common ground with a not-so-positive woman. By the time they arrived at the airport, they were buddies. Judy hugged my friend and said, "Listen, if you ever come to town again and need a ride anywhere — you call me. I'd be delighted to help you any way I can."

My friend found common ground that day and new opportunities were opened to her for the future. She made a friend in that city, but more important, she showed love, respect, and kindness to a woman who probably doesn't encounter that very often.

When you are considerate and listen to others, it's amazing what you'll discover about them, even when you thought you knew them so well! Moreover, when you show kindness and mercy toward someone, God can give you wisdom and new insights about that person. He'll help you understand her better so you can be more compassionate. Let's not be quick to share our opinions and cut people off, because you never know when God is trying to bring you into a divine connection.

My brother, Don, was out looking for a new car and thought he found the one he wanted. The salesman was going to get him some additional information, so Don gave the man his phone number to call him later on. Several days passed, and Don changed his mind about that particular car.

A couple of nights later, Don had just come home after a long day at work and sat down to a wonderful hot bowl of noodle soup — his favorite on a cold night. He was just starting to relax and was ready to dig in when his daughter came running over with the phone. "Daddy, Daddy! There's someone on the phone for you."

Reluctantly Don took the call, only to discover it was the salesperson from the car dealership. As soon as he said hello, the salesperson started going on and on about that car Don had looked at more than a week ago. Don was trying to be as nice as possible and said, "Thank you, but I've decided that car is not big enough, and I have changed my mind." The salesman went on and on about how great the car was, as if he hadn't even heard what Don said. Don just sat there staring at that big bowl of noodles getting colder and colder, trying to be as nice as possible.

"Sir, I've changed my mind about that car."

The man continued to try to talk Don into the car. "Would you like to talk with my sales manager?" he asked.

Don took a deep breath and had several phrases rolling around in his head when suddenly he heard himself say yes. Immediately he thought, *Did I just say yes?* During the brief moment of silence, he kept reminding himself to be nice and courteous even though all he really wanted to do was to enjoy his dinner.

The manager got on the phone and introduced himself and said, "I just want to ask you a question."

"Thank you," Don replied, "but really, I've changed my mind about that —"

The manager interrupted. "Are you Victoria Osteen's brother?" he asked.

"Yes," Don responded.

The manager continued, "I go to Lakewood Church, and even if you don't want that particular car, I want to help you find the car you want and get you the very best price possible."

Don was pleasantly surprised. And because he was determined to keep peace and be kind and courteous, God was able to bring him a divine connection. Several weeks later, the sales manager found Don the car he really wanted and gave him a price he could hardly believe.

Had Don flatly told the salesman, "I am sitting down to dinner and can't be bothered right now," that would have been the end of the conversation and Don's blessing would have gone unfulfilled. When we are willing to be patient and listen to others, even when we don't feel like it, the results will always be positive and will far outweigh the inconvenience.

Regardless of whether we are dealing with our spouses, our children, or a salesman on the phone, we should always strive to show others that we respect them and value them. Our relationships will thrive when we live considerately and look for the common ground that unites us.

ANCHOR THOUGHTS

I will study the people in my life and find out what they need. I will look for ways to support them and make their lives easier, focusing on giving them what they need and not what I need.

I will be willing to make adjustments and adapt my plans and my ways to show respect and bring more harmony to my home. I will be sensitive to the needs of others and recognize what makes them happy. I realize minor adjustments can make major differences.

I realize that as I meet other people's needs, God will meet my needs.

When people talk to me, I will honor them and let them know how valuable they are by giving them my full attention.

I will look for ways to find common ground with the people in my life. I will focus on what we agree on and not allow our disagreements to separate us. I will not push my point of view, but let others be heard for the sake of peace.

10
BEING A PEOPLE BUILDER

When I was a child, I remember learning about the Golden Rule: Do unto others as you would have them do unto you. The Golden Rule is still a great place to begin in our relationships. I recently read a children's book that put a new twist on the old adage. The premise of the story was that we each carry an invisible bucket — yes, we all have one! It's an emotional bucket, and when your bucket is full you feel happy, satisfied, and encouraged; when your bucket is empty, you feel down and discouraged. In this world, there are "bucket fillers" and "bucket dippers." A bucket filler is a person who adds to other people by encouraging and investing in them with kind words and actions. When bucket fillers are investing in others, they find that their own buckets are filled up, too. Bucket dippers, on the other hand, are those who take away from people by using harsh or negative words. They not only deplete other people's buckets but also diminish the contents of their own.

God intends for us to be bucket fillers, using our lives and resources to help people be the very best they can be. I think about Peter, one of the disciples of Jesus. He was impulsive; he said things he shouldn't have and he needed to grow in a lot of areas. Despite Peter's personality drawbacks, Jesus referred to him in surprisingly positive terms. He said, "Peter, you are a rock." Simon Peter's very name meant "pebble," and I wonder if he felt like a tiny pebble at times, especially after some of his foolish blunders. Nevertheless, Jesus reminded Peter of what he was becoming — a solid, stable rock. He spoke potential and confidence into Peter's life, and we should follow that example in our relationships. Let's be bucket fillers, not bucket dippers. Let's not remind the people in our lives of their failures and faults; instead, let's see the solid rock in them and speak positively about what they are becoming.

What are you doing to fill the buckets of the loved ones in your life? Whether you are a natural encourager or you feel a bit uncomfortable giving compliments, you possess a unique ability to make others feel better about themselves. The truth is, we all have different personalities and different ways of relating to one another, but we can all become great encouragers. I truly believe encouragement is one of the best gifts we can give other people. The Scripture tells us to "Encourage one another daily."

Throughout the day, we have opportunities to get discouraged. We face difficulties; plans don't always work out; and life has a way of stealing our joy. That's why we need to get in the habit of encouraging one another daily. Every one of us needs his or her emotional bucket to be filled up and refilled on a regular basis. A simple compliment or a kind word can make someone's day!

Not only do positive words lift up others, but I've found that encouraging words are the glue that holds our relationships together. Looking back over the last twenty-one years in my marriage, I can see how positive words and regular affirmations have bonded Joel's and my heart together and have caused us to bring out the best in each other. We've learned the importance of encouraging each other daily — not just through our words, but through simple acts of kindness and finding ways to make life easier for each other. You can do the same in your relationships, and I believe it will improve the atmosphere of your household, your workplace, your community, and your world.

Sure, it takes effort to be a great encourager, but when you take time to encourage someone, that investment will eventually yield a good return. When you bring out the best in others and help them succeed, that success *will* come back to you and cause you to rise higher, as well. Start encouraging someone today with your words and actions, and you, too, can rise to new levels. When you fill the emotional buckets of others, God will make sure to fill your bucket.

SUCCESS BREEDS SUCCESS

It's important to recognize that the people closest to you need to hear your words of encouragement. Sometimes we compliment strangers or people we barely know more than we compliment our own family members. We'll tell a coworker what a great job she did, but when our spouse excels, we don't say a word. Or when our children look nice, we're so used to it that we overlook them and miss that chance to encourage, but when we see a coworker wearing a new outfit, we're quick to tell her how great she looks. We should compliment and encourage our own family members as much as we do others.

It's easy to take the people closest to us for granted. "I don't need to say anything to them," you might say. "They know I love them. She knows I think she is beautiful. He knows I think he is a great." But a blessing is not a blessing until it is spoken. When you release those positive words of affirmation, they will have a positive effect in the lives of the people you love. Your spouse, your children, and the ones you associate with day in and day out need to hear your words of approval and affirmation more than anyone else. Don't take the people God has given you for granted. Have you said "I love you" to your spouse today? Have you told your children how much they mean to you? Are you looking for opportunities to compliment and encourage those *closest* to you? I am convinced that when we put family first, when we take the time and make the effort to be good to our family members and give them our best, then all the other relationships in our lives will improve as well.

I heard about a woman who said to her husband one day, "Honey, do you really love me?"

He looked at her strangely and said, "Why would you ask me that? I told you that I loved you the day I married you thirty-five years ago. If it ever changes, I'll let you know."

Let's not allow that to be us. Every day we should tell the people in our lives how much we love them and never tire of expressing our appreciation. It will make a difference — I promise.

I grew up in a home where we were constantly saying "I love you." It became very normal, just a part of our everyday conversation. When we would leave the house or hang up the phone, we would always say "I love you." To this day, my older brother still says those words to me, and we are both carrying on that tradition in our own families. Every time our children hang up the phone with Joel or me, it's just natural for them to say "I love you." That principle has been deposited in their hearts, and now they are comfortable with those words. Joel and I lead by example and hopefully Alexandra and Jonathan will carry on this tradition of love in their families.

The phrase "I love you" can never be heard enough in our homes. Are there those close to you who need to hear those words? Begin to say them today. Maybe you weren't raised in this kind of expressive environment, but why don't you be the one to start a new tradition? You can affect your family line for generations to come. What better legacy to leave than a legacy of love, kindness, and encouragement?

People often compliment Joel after he speaks, saying something like "Joel, that message was really great. You've helped change my life." Those are meaningful words of encouragement for him, but I have learned they don't have nearly as much impact on Joel as when I offer my words of affirmation. As a spouse, as a family member, recognize your words carry greater weight. Sometimes I'll look over at Joel on Sunday evening and say, "Joel, you're always good, but that message was especially great today." I know how important it is to recognize his hard work and dedication, so often I will mention a specific point I liked in his message. I can see how that encourages him and lets him know I appreciate his gifts and talents. Even though he may have heard numerous compliments from other people that day, as his wife, my words have more impact. They take deeper root because God designed it that way.

On the other hand, when you don't use your words to compliment and encourage, you're not taking advantage of the gift God has given you. And in the end, it affects not only you but the other people in your life as well. They may never rise as high as they should unless you speak words of faith and victory over them. Remember, the higher we help others go, the higher we will go. We have a responsibility to use our words to encourage. So if you want to love your life, express your love and encouragement to those who are close to you.

I've always seen great things in Joel. Before he ever thought he could minister, I used to tell him, "One day you are going to pastor this church." Sure, we were sitting in the front row, listening to Joel's father preach, but I visualized Joel up there one day. I could see that talent in him. Joel would get aggravated and say, "Don't tell me that, Victoria. I don't know how to preach."

I would tease him, "Sure you do, Joel. Just preach to them like you preach to me!" Not only could I see it in him, but I released my faith by saying it to him. Understand, Joel liked being behind the scenes. He's naturally more quiet and reserved. Yet somehow as his wife, I was given insight by God and just knew that someday Joel was going to be up on that platform; I knew it was going to happen. I wasn't trying to pressure him. I wasn't trying to talk him into it. I simply knew it in my heart, so I did my best to encourage him and speak faith into him. To this day, Joel says that a major reason he was able to take over for his father after Daddy Osteen went to heaven was because he had heard me tell him so many times what I saw in him, and how I believed he could do it. There was a confidence and a boldness that was planted inside Joel, and those seeds took root and burst forth at just the right time. Joel rose up in faith and stepped out, and God has done more than we could ask or think.

You have the power to speak words of faith and victory into your family, and you must recognize the weight your words carry and the influence you have on those closest to you.

The people in our inner circle not only *want* our approval — they *need* it. I was discussing the power of encouragement with one of my friends one afternoon and she said something I thought was right on. She shared, "When I brag on my husband, I can see a change in him. He rises to the occasion and strives to go to new levels. But when I nag at him or say nothing at all, he's more complacent and doesn't have the passion and enthusiasm to accomplish what is in his heart."

That's true for all of us. Nagging only makes things worse, but encouraging words put people on their feet and bring out the best in them. Make the most of opportunities to speak good things into the lives of the people around you. When your spouse gets a promotion at work, take time to say, "I knew you could do it! You're amazing!" When your child comes home with good grades, even if they are less than *you* had hoped, don't be too busy to celebrate. Stop and say, "I am so proud of you. Way to go!" When your mother fixes Sunday dinner for the whole family, tell her, "Mom, I know that's a lot of work, but your hospitality means so much." When your coworker loses fifteen pounds, don't be jealous; congratulate her with a compliment.

We need to look for opportunities to use our words to build up the people in our lives. Rather than condemning people for what they are doing wrong, let's strive to catch people doing things right — and compliment and reward them with encouraging words. Your words of affirmation can draw people close to you and add value to them. Use your words to build someone's confidence and watch what happens!

With our words we can help people see the best in themselves. If your sister is really good at organization, encourage her to use that talent. You might say, "You are such a great organizer. In fact, you could probably make a business out of your organizational skills. I'd hire you for sure!" That simple expression of encouragement could cause your sister to believe in herself and go for her dreams. Be that cheerleader in her life. Constantly be on the lookout for opportunities to fill the emotional buckets of those in your life. Encourage them in their gifts and talents, and watch them go to the next level.

Understand, this form of encouragement is not generic. To be effective, we have to take time to identify specific strengths in people and build on those with our words. Specific encouragement, however, doesn't need to be intrusive; it might include something as simple as acknowledging someone in an honorable manner.

Years ago, a friend was visiting me from another state and during her stay, I introduced her to some of my friends and family, including the husband of a well-known lady in the community — a woman who is regularly on television and often the center of attention. When I introduced her husband, I purposely didn't introduce him as this woman's husband. Instead, I introduced him by name and then simply stated that *she* was married to him. I noticed the pleased surprise on his face. He put his shoulders back and seemed to enjoy the fact that someone recognized who he was and took the time to make him feel important. Just that little change of emphasis can make all the difference. It showed him respect and let him know that I valued him for who he was — not just as a well-known person's husband. Be sensitive and go out of your way to express respect in specific ways, and you will be pleasantly surprised at the results.

Another way to fill someone's emotional bucket is by doing small acts of kindness for him or her. We all like different things, or to put it another way, we don't all like the same things. Find out what makes the people in your life feel special. It doesn't have to be something big that takes weeks of planning and costs a lot of money — a cruise, a diamond ring, a swimming pool. That's all great, but don't wait for the big things to bless the people in your life. I've found that small acts of kindness often have just as much or even more impact. Joel knows that I love one cup of coffee every morning. What's interesting is that Joel doesn't drink coffee, but because he knows *I* love it, he takes time to make it for me every day. And quite often he even brings it to me in bed! Usually Joel gets up earlier than I do, and when I go into the kitchen and see my coffee already made, that lets me know that Joel was thinking about me. When he got up, I was on his mind. That's something that doesn't take him two minutes. It's not hard; it's not expensive; yet it lets me know how important I am to him and how much he loves me. That small act of kindness goes a long way with me.

Sometimes we wait to plan big, extravagant events to express our love and appreciation, forgetting that little things mean the most. Small acts of kindness performed on a regular basis make a much bigger impact on people's lives. I like a quote I found from Aesop that says, "No act of kindness, no matter how small, is ever wasted."

What acts of kindness can you do today? When you drive through and get that morning cup of coffee and a muffin, why not pick up an extra muffin for a coworker or your boss? If you know your friend collects magnets from different states, why not pick up a few as you drive to your next vacation destination? Those thoughtful little gestures of encouragement leave big smiles on the faces of our loved ones.

Try alleviating some of the pressure on your loved ones this week by putting actions to your encouragement. If your spouse is about to go on a business trip, why not pick up his dry cleaning for him so he won't have to make that extra stop? If your best friend has recently embarked on a new fitness program, why not offer to watch her children one night this week so she can take that class at the gym?

Maybe you are a person of few words, and you are far too shy to encourage someone through verbal communication — that's okay. Did you know that you say much by your nonverbal cues? In fact, one study at UCLA stated that up to 93 percent of communication effectiveness is determined by nonverbal cues. That means you can encourage people by simply flashing your pearly whites. People can't always read your mind, but they can definitely read your face. That's why I always make it a point to smile at my children when we make eye contact. They usually return my smile and show me their gorgeous grins. I love that! Sometimes a smile is all you need.

I once heard a famous speaker sharing about this very topic. He said he speaks in front of thousands of people every year, and sometimes he gets applause and other times he doesn't. But none of that moves him in the least as long as he can look down to the front row and see his beautiful wife gazing up at him and smiling with great admiration and approval. That familiar smile is all the encouragement he needs to finish his speech.

I am also conscious of my impact on Joel when he looks down and sees me sitting in the front row of Lakewood Church. That's why I laugh just as hard at his opening joke the third time I've heard it that weekend as I did during the very first service. It's important to encourage with our smiles, and it's such an easy thing to do. Try it! The next time you are in a business meeting and your boss is making a presentation, flash a supportive smile her way. Couple that smile with a nod when your boss makes her key points, and you've become the best encourager in the room.

Those simple words, gestures, and actions of encouragement can totally change the atmosphere of your household and touch the hearts of those you love. And here's a real bonus — filling the emotional buckets of others will have a positive effect on you, too! I've noticed that when I encourage others, it reminds me of the great people I have in my life, and it causes my heart to be grateful. Encouraging others keeps my mind focused on the good things each person possesses and not the negative things. It's easy to take our blessings for granted, but when we encourage one another, we remind ourselves how blessed we are to have such wonderful people surrounding us. Each time you offer a word of encouragement, you're creating a grateful heart and a right mind-set within yourself. Everybody benefits from encouragement — that's the way God designed it.

Did you know that words have creative power? When God created the heavens and the earth, He spoke them into existence. We are made in His image and our words have creative power, too. I like to think of it like this: We are all artists with our words and we paint on the canvas of people's hearts with every word we speak, good or bad. That's why we need to be careful to use our words wisely, as a skillful artist would, creating a positive, encouraging masterpiece in the hearts of our family members, friends, and coworkers. And a beautiful work of art isn't created merely by choosing the right colors of paint; it's created by the technique the artist uses. In the same way, we have to be careful *how* we communicate to the people around us.

I learned this lesson the hard way when I was trying to encourage Jonathan to practice his guitar. I was driving the kids home from school one day and thinking about all of the loose ends I'd left dangling on that particular afternoon. You might say I was feeling a bit stressed, and I let that stress come right through my words when I sharply asked, "Jonathan, have you practiced your guitar at all this week?"

Before he could answer, I continued, "You know, if you don't practice your guitar now, you'll be sorry down the road when you want to play in the band at church and you're not good enough." On and on I went, trying to encourage my eleven-year-old son to practice his guitar with enthusiasm and passion, and yet I could see his countenance deflating and becoming more discouraged by the minute. All at once, I could hear my words. They weren't encouraging or inspiring. They were negative and depressing. I realized that I was painting a negative picture on the canvas of his heart.

Immediately I stopped myself and said, "Jonathan, I'm sorry. I realize I wasn't very encouraging just now. Will you forgive me?"

I looked at him in the rearview mirror, and he just smiled at me so sweetly. Right then, I decided to use my words to paint a positive image. I mentally put away the negativity paintbrush and reached for the encouraging brush and said, "You are so talented musically. That's why I want you to practice, because I know the more you practice, the better you'll become . . ." I changed my voice from the voice of discouragement and defeat to the voice of encouragement and victory.

When we realize the impact of our words, we'll seize every opportunity to paint positive images on the hearts of those we love. We'll look for chances to say, "I'm behind you. I'm supporting you. I'm with you every step of the way."

Just like anything else, it will take practice to become a skillful "painter" with your words, but you can do it! Even when you have to bring correction or instruction, you can position your words so they will be more easily received. They say that "a spoonful of sugar helps the medicine go down," and when you speak words of affirmation along with the correction, it makes it much more palatable. Whether you're a boss working with an employee or a parent working with a child, the goal should always be to help others reach a higher level. When we communicate the value of making the change, it will be easier for the person to receive it. Don't allow harsh words to cut the canvas you are working on! Instead, "sweeten" your delivery with words of affirmation.

A few years ago, I was deeply engaged in conversation with a woman while Alexandra was standing right beside me and really wanted my attention. This woman was pouring her heart out to me, and I didn't want to cut her off midsentence, but by this time Alexandra was tugging on my pant leg, desperate for my attention.

I started to get frustrated with my little girl, but instead I decided to make a positive deposit into her heart. I interrupted the woman very respectfully and said, "Just one minute. I need to speak with my daughter, but I really want to hear the rest of your story." Then I knelt down beside Alexandra and looked attentively into her big blue eyes and whispered, "I know you want to talk to me right now, but I am already speaking with this woman and I can't listen to both of you at the same time. Honey, what you have to say is so important to me, I don't want to miss one single word of it, so give me two minutes to finish up, and I'll give you my full attention."

Alexandra smiled at me and nodded in agreement. In fact, her whole body language changed because she felt important. She stood a little taller and prouder after I had whispered those words to her. That deposit in her life let her know how much she mattered to me. She knew that she would have her mother's undivided attention in a few minutes, and she was content to wait for me.

That's how we build the people around us. It seems like such a little thing, but those little deposits will eventually make a big difference. Over time, those little deposits of encouragement will create a winning attitude inside a person's heart.

Maybe no one took the time to invest in you this way when you were growing up, but if you listen carefully, God is constantly speaking words of affirmation into your heart. He created you to be a winner, and He wants to help you learn to communicate that message to the people around you. It's never too late to change how you communicate!

Have you ever heard the expression "More is caught than taught"? This is especially true with our children. We have to be very careful what we say and do in front of them. They are like little sponges, absorbing every word that comes out of our mouths and imitating our every action. I have a friend who is Southern through and through, and she has a four-year-old daughter who looks exactly like her. She told me the story of how one day her daughter came bounding into the kitchen, saying, "I've got FIRE in me! I've got FIRE in me!" My friend looked at her daughter and said, "What fire are you talking about? Who told you, you have fire in you?" Her little girl continued running around saying it all day, and it really bothered my friend. She was concerned that someone would tell her precious daughter that she had fire in her, and she wondered what that meant.

A few days later, my friend told me how she caught herself saying, "Girl, I'm going to spank the *fire* out of you," just as her mother had said to her. It was an old Southern phrase, and she would never do anything to harm her child. Even though it was a funny story and we got a chuckle, it made a tremendous point. It is amazing what we can deposit with our words into the hearts and minds of the people we love.

Recognize that someone is always watching and listening to you. That's why we must live our lives with purpose and resolve, so we can challenge those around us to rise higher. Our words are painting pictures in the hearts of those we love, and we can create masterpieces with every stroke.

LIVING WITH WINNERS

I was speaking with a friend and her husband the other day. She was jokingly telling me, "In my house, I am always right."

Her husband chimed in, "She lives to be right! She challenges everything we say," referring to himself and their children.

"He just hates that I'm always right," she said with a big smile on her face.

This could have been funny, if it were not for the fact that she wasn't kidding. She didn't recognize that her desire to be right all the time was causing those around her to feel wrong all the time. If you always have to win, then that makes you the only champion in your house. And that's not good. Her need to be right was creating a losing environment for her husband and children. She was depleting their sense of worth and value, and she didn't even realize it.

Sometimes you have to know when to let things go, even though you may think you are right. If you never let your spouse or your children win a debate or even a simple game of Monopoly, you're creating a spirit of defeat on the inside of them. Eventually your family will just quit trying and lose that passion to win.

I want to live with winners. I have learned that I don't have to win every discussion with Joel because ultimately, if he wins, I win. We're a team! That's how you have to see the situation when your mind is screaming, "I want to be right!" Let your spouse be a winner, because then you'll be married to a champion, and that is a win-win situation any way you look at it.

It's important that you team up with your spouse and those who are close to you to help their dreams become reality. But make sure that your words of encouragement are backed up with action on your part. Don't place all the pressure on them by failing to do your share.

I knew a woman who was trying to encourage her husband and would always say, "You are going to make a million dollars!" Although she was trying to speak faith into his heart and encourage him, day after day, those words felt like pressure to him. She completely put the burden on his shoulders and he was overwhelmed with the heavy load.

Any time I encouraged Joel that we could do something in our lives, I was right there with him, willing to do my part. If we had a financial goal, I did my part to save money. If we were remodeling a house, I was in the yard laying sod. When we were building a home, I was there every day to meet the subcontractors and help keep us on schedule. When he became pastor of the church, I did my part in the service, too! Joel and I are a team, and the best way to show I support him is by rolling up my sleeves with him!

I encourage you today: Don't put the load of responsibilities for your happiness on your spouse or the people around you. Make the decision to do your part. When you fill the emotional buckets of others, you enable them to do the same for you.

Strive each day to be a people builder and help make those people around you a group of winners. Success breeds success, and when you encourage others in their dreams, you are not only building great relationships, but you are setting the stage to bring your own goals and dreams to pass.

ANCHOR THOUGHTS

I will make a habit of giving someone the gift of encouragement every day. I recognize if I don't use my words to compliment and encourage, I'm not taking advantage of the gift God has given me.

I realize how much weight my words carry and I will seize every opportunity to paint positive pictures on the hearts of those I love.

I will always remember that no act of kindness is ever too small or ever wasted when I am depositing it in someone else's life.

I will help those closest to me to succeed. I will compliment my spouse, speak faith into my children, and build up my family. I realize that success breeds success, and the higher they go, the higher I will go.

I will enjoy the words "I love you" and allow them to flow freely in my home. I will not assume people know how I feel about them; instead I will tell them on a regular basis.

I will show my love through small acts of kindness. I will look for ways to let my family know that I'm thinking of them. I realize that it's the little things done frequently that keep my relationships strong.

11
Receiving Love

In this day and age, the word "love" can be used in just about any context. We love our family or soul mate, and we also love a good movie or *pizza!* It's no wonder people get so confused about the subject of love. One thing is certain: Every person on this earth was created with a deep longing to give and receive love. We develop our personal definition of love by how we were raised and what we saw modeled in our homes growing up. Whether they realize it or not, most people have a picture of God in their minds based on what their relationship was like with their natural father. If their earthly father was kind and supportive, it's easy to see God the same way. On the other hand, if their earthly father was unavailable or distant, they may find it difficult to see the unconditional love that God so freely gives.

I grew up in a home where the phrase "I love you" was as natural as the word "hello."

To this day, if you are around my family for very long, you will hear those three little words, because we look for opportunities to express our love to one another. I realize that it's easy for me to accept God's love because of the way I was raised. I had a great childhood, with a loving brother and a fantastic mom and dad who believed in me, encouraged me, and loved me, even if I did something wrong (which I rarely did, of course!). My parents never judged me by my performance. My mother instilled within me a sense of independence and confidence that I could do anything I put my mind to. My father loved and protected me, and would pick me up when I fell. My parents were always good to me and showed me their unconditional love and approval. But I still had to learn to embrace that love. At times I had to let go of my own way of doing things, because *occasionally* my way wasn't exactly the best way.

I can remember when I was sixteen years old, my dad would allow me to drive the family car to the grocery store. "Go straight to the store, get the groceries, and then come straight back home," he would say. "Don't pick up any of your friends, just go, and come back."

One day as I was headed for the store, my

dad cautioned me, "Victoria, the passenger-side window is off its track. Please don't open the passenger-side door, and especially don't lower the passenger-side window. I have an appointment to get it repaired, but for right now, just don't lower it."

"Okay, Dad," I said with a kiss and a smile as I headed out the door. And as any good sixteen-year-old girl would do, I went straight to my best friend's house down the street and picked her up, and we headed to the grocery store together. Being the responsible young lady that I was, I told her to be careful about the window. Well, we drove barely one block when we saw a friend of ours walking down the street. Of course, we weren't trying to impress him or anything or show off the fact that I was driving; we just wanted to innocently say hi.

"Just go ahead and roll down the window and say hello to him," I told my friend.

"But I thought your dad said not to lower the window," she hedged.

Caught up in the moment, I said, "Oh, it will be okay. Just do it slowly."

My friend rolled down the window and we called out to our friend, waving and acting so grown up. He seemed so impressed that I was driving, and my friend and I acted as cool as could be. Everything was great until my friend started to raise the window. Suddenly it seemed like the world stopped as I watched the window crack and shatter into a million pieces! I would have given anything to turn back the clock at that moment.

"Oh, no!" I cried. "You have to come home with me and help me explain to my dad what happened," I told my friend. Suddenly the groceries didn't seem so important anymore. We drove straight back home in complete silence. The walk up our driveway wasn't nearly long enough as I tried to figure out how to explain to my dad what just happened. I walked inside, along with my friend — the one who wasn't supposed to be with me. My dad was in the kitchen making some hamburgers when he turned and saw us. You can imagine the puzzled look on his face. "Dad, I'm so sorry . . . ," I started to say, barely knowing how to explain what had happened.

Because I knew my father loved me, I had the confidence to tell him the whole story. And the marvelous part is that the moment I admitted to my dad that I had disobeyed, he forgave me. Of course he was disappointed, but he never ceased to love me. He didn't hold it over my head or measure my worth by that mistake. He chose to believe the best about me. In fact, his love for me was just as strong after that incident as before. He never disconnected his heart from mine and I did not retreat from his love. Our relationship continued to flourish as it does to this day. My dad is as proud of me as any father could be.

Maybe you weren't raised in a family like mine and it's hard for you to believe that God is so forgiving. Maybe it's time for you to redefine what you know as love. God's love goes way beyond any human love you've ever experienced. He is always patient and kind, always just and forgiving. He weeps when you weep and laughs when you laugh. You are His delight and He longs to have a loving relationship with you. You bring joy to His heart and I know He is smiling on you right now as you read these words.

I encounter so many people who have a misconception that God is always mad at them. When things don't go well, the first thing they say is "Well, God, You did it to me again!" It's as if they think God is just waiting for them to do something wrong so He can punish them and make their lives difficult. Let me assure you right now, that is the furthest thing from the truth! *God is not mad at you; He is madly in love with you!*

To truly love your life, you must understand and embrace this fundamental truth.

It doesn't matter how many times you've made a mistake; it doesn't matter how many times you've blown it; God is always ready to receive you with open, loving arms. In fact, He's already forgiven you for anything you've done in the past and anything you will do in the future. All you must do is accept it. Imagine God in front of you right now with His arms outstretched, ready to welcome you. Don't run away from Him; run toward Him. Simply take a step of faith to embrace His love and forgiveness.

Studies show that children grow and flourish when they are approved, accepted, and valued. But when a child is raised in an environment that is harsh and disapproving, when he feels like he can't be good enough, it limits his self-esteem.

A survey done for a national magazine revealed that 59 percent of CEOs are firstborn children. I don't find this surprising when you consider how most firstborn children are treated by their parents — everything those children do is so amazing! That first smile, that first word, that first step — each first is seen as the most magnificent event of the year. Even most grandparents marvel at and encourage every move of that firstborn child. That constant recognition of every small achievement builds confidence and security.

Did you know God sees you the same way? Regardless of whether you were the firstborn in your family or not, you are the apple of God's eye. He will always treat you like His most valuable child. He applauds you every time you take a step of faith. He's always speaking encouraging words into your heart, saying, "You can rise higher. You can do all things. You can fulfill your destiny."

Let those words sink down into your heart and allow them to build your confidence. When you understand and receive God's love and encouragement, it will empower you to do more than you ever thought possible. Because of God's love and constant support, you can wake up every day with an attitude of faith and expectancy. You don't have to live guilty or condemned, feeling like you don't measure up. You may have made some mistakes, but just like a parent helps a child when he is learning to walk, God will help you get right back up any time you fall. Do your part, and instead of dwelling on all you did wrong the day before, just imagine God smiling down on you. It's very freeing to say, "God is pleased with me. God approves of me." Embrace these words and let them create a foundation of His unconditional love in your life. Remember, you are His most prized possession, the apple of His eye!

Have you ever wondered what God thinks about, what is on His mind? It says in Psalms that God is mindful *of us.* That means God is constantly thinking about you and me. What does He think about us? Is He thinking about our mistakes, our failures, or our shortcomings? No, God's thoughts toward us are good! He's not thinking about what we did wrong, He's thinking about what we did right. He's not thinking about how far we have to go; He's thinking about how far we've come. God approves of you. He's pleased with you. It's time to start approving of yourself.

When Jesus walked the earth, He left us two simple commands: Love God and love your neighbor *as you love yourself.*[18] Notice it doesn't just say, "Love God and people." No, it says love others as you love *yourself.* That means you can never love anyone until you love yourself first. Loving yourself is not about being selfish; it's about honoring God's creation . . . *you!*

I encourage you today to receive God's

love in a new way. Ask Him to show you His unconditional love. When you understand His true love, you'll be set free from any kind of inferiority and insecurity. You become more grounded and better able to love others as you love yourself. The more we accept God's love, the more love we will be able to give in return — both to Him and to the people who matter the most to us.

LOVE BUILDS SECURITY

Joel and I have been married for more than twenty-one years, and the strength of our relationship comes from the unconditional love we have for each other. We do not love each other just when things are good or when we agree on everything; no, we are committed to loving each other no matter what.

Even though I know Joel loves me and we make a conscious effort to invest in each other, every day is certainly not a perfect day. There are those days when we don't meet each other's expectations. But when things don't go the right way, I don't look at what I've done, I look at what I know — that I am loved unconditionally. We have to remember to go back to the foundation of love in our relationships, especially in our

275

relationship with God. The thing that keeps me most stable is the knowledge that because God loves me, I am empowered to do better. I am strongest when I build my days on the foundation of His love for me.

It's important that we learn to be comfortable with telling the people in our lives that we love them. We need to allow these words to flow freely in our homes to create an atmosphere of love. At the same time, we need to be comfortable hearing those words spoken to us in return. I know Joel loves me, but I still like to hear him say it on a regular basis. Sure, they are just three little words, but I allow them to sink deep down in my heart every time I hear them. I know that when I embrace those words, they establish a treasure of security and trust in my heart. I rely on Joel's love and allow it to sink deep into my being, because in any good relationship, love has to be the anchor that keeps us steady through the tough times.

We all have a memory box inside our hearts. We can either record all the hurts and difficulties in our relationships or we can allow God's love to wipe the pages clean so we can record the good. When the tough times come, whatever is recorded in our heart will manifest in our lives. Joel and I always remind ourselves that God brought us together, and we go back to our memory box and review that over and over again. That is how we keep our relationship anchored — by focusing on all the great times we've shared together and the future that's in front of us.

If you have some books filled with photos or family fun, take an evening away from the television or work and simply enjoy going through some of those old pictures, reminding yourself and your loved ones of the great things God has done for you. Enjoy them with your spouse, children, or friends, and remind yourselves how much you love one another. It's so important that we take the steps to recognize our love for one another and keep it alive.

A young woman heard me speaking on this subject and wrote to tell me how much she appreciated my encouragement to embrace those words "I love you."

"I really want to embrace my husband's love," she said, "but I get so down on myself and feel like I'm not good enough for my husband. I feel like I'm apologizing to him all the time and don't measure up to what he needs." She admitted that her personal feelings of inadequacy were driving a wedge in their relationship by allowing her thoughts of failure to feed insecurity into her heart and mind. In her own thinking, their relationship was getting stuck and not progressing the way she felt it should. She knew her husband loved her, but she couldn't embrace his love. It was as if she couldn't get beyond her own mistakes for fear of her husband's rejection. He truly loved her, but her feelings of inadequacy were not allowing her to receive his love and to grow and mature in that love.

It wasn't until she adjusted her own thinking that their relationship was rescued from that rut and began progressing toward renewed love and trust.

I think we do something similar in our relationship with God when we don't allow His love and acceptance to give us a sense of security, and to cover our failures. God's love is not based on our performance, but when we recognize and embrace His love, it will improve our performance. His love builds trust in our heart, so we are free to improve our lives and become all we were created to be. His love frees us to work with ourselves, not just to work on ourselves. It causes us to want to know Him better, and to want to know ourselves better. His love is what motivates us to be our absolute best.

In the New Testament, you'll find a story

about a woman who was caught in the act of adultery. The religious leaders had already condemned her in their minds, because their law said she should be stoned. Out of curiosity, they brought her to Jesus to see what He would do, but Jesus surprised them all with His response. He didn't condemn the woman, but instead He showed love and compassion to her. In fact, He turned the whole thing around and said, "You who are without sin, throw the first stone."[19] The accusers left one by one.

Jesus turned to the woman and said, "Where are your accusers? Did anyone condemn you?"

She answered, "No one, Lord."

Jesus then said something very profound, something that gives us insight into who He really is: "Neither do I condemn you. Go and sin no more." God was in essence saying, "I don't put my stamp of approval on condemnation." God is not in the business of condemning people; He's in the business of improving and loving people.

You may have encountered people who want to accuse you and throw rocks at you. But that's not the way our God is. He's never going to throw rocks at you or try to push you down. He wants to empower you to live a better life. Maybe you've made

279

some mistakes, or maybe you've been hurt by someone who threw rocks at you. Today is your day to let go of that hurt and open your heart to receive God's love.

Remember, as long as we live, there will be accusing voices. The faultfinders and rock throwers will always be there. When the negative voices come, we can believe them and stay where we are, or we can believe that we're forgiven, accepted, and approved by God. It's up to us to cast the deciding vote as to what is going to dominate our lives — freedom or condemnation, faith or fear, love or bitterness. Decide today to make the best choice. Receive God's love. Get up every morning and declare it, "God loves me. God approves of me." When you accept yourself, you honor God. As you learn to receive God's love, you'll not only love your life more, but you'll have plenty of love to give away.

My prayer for you today is that you will love your life in a greater way, that you will understand your value and what you have to offer, that you will live with confidence, making the most of what God has given you, and that you will see God's favor in a greater way.

Make sure your memory box is filled with the right things. You have so much to offer.

All through the day remind yourself that you are a person of destiny, handpicked by Almighty God. Treasure the people in your life. Be willing to make adjustments to improve your relationships. Don't hold on to offenses. Keep the connections strong. The difficulty may be for a season, but your relationship is for a lifetime. And when times get tough keep the right perspective. Remember, you can always choose the *God option.* Your hands may be tied, but God's hands are never tied. Trust Him. Live each day in faith. Focus on what you have and not on what you don't have. If you'll put on a fresh new attitude each morning, treasuring the people in your life, recognizing your possibilities and living with confidence, you will see God's favor and blessings and you will live your life happy, healthy, and whole.

GOD IS NOT MAD AT YOU — HE IS MADLY IN LOVE WITH YOU

Joel and I love you and pray for you every day. If you've never accepted the love and forgiveness that Jesus has to offer, let me encourage you to do so. I'm not talking about becoming religious and trying to be good enough, I'm talking about having a relationship with the Creator of the universe through His son Jesus Christ. It's so simple. Just pray this prayer in your heart: "Dear Jesus, I know I'm a sinner and I need a savior. I believe You are the son of God, that You died paying the price for my sins, and rose again. I ask You to come into my life, make me fresh and new. I accept You as my Lord and Savior." As you prayed that prayer, I believe today is a new beginning. Let go of the old and receive the new. We would love to help you. Visit our website at www-.joelosteen.com for more information. When you're in Houston, stop by and see us. We love you, believe in you, and know that your best days are out in front of you.

ANCHOR THOUGHTS

Today I am receiving God's love. I know His mercy is fresh and new every morning, and I'm going to fill my memory box with the treasures from God's Word and live this day with faith and expectancy.

I know that I'm approved, accepted, and valued in the eyes of God. I know God is not mad at me. He's madly in love with me.

No matter how many mistakes I've made or how many times I've blown it, I believe God's love never changes, and He is always there with open arms to receive me.

I realize that God's love for me is not based on my performance, but as I recognize it and embrace it, His love improves my performance.

If someone is throwing rocks, I know it's not God. He's not in the business of condemning, He's in the business of loving. I will not live this day guilty and condemned. I have been forgiven from all past mistakes. This is a new day of victory.

NOTES

1. The names of all persons other than family members and public figures mentioned in this book are pseudonyms.
2. See Esther 2:1–8:27.
3. See 1 Samuel 16:1–13.
4. See Matthew 5:16.
5. See 2 Timothy 1:5.
6. See Numbers 13:1–14:24.
7. See Joshua 1:1–9.
8. See 1 Samuel 17:12–54.
9. See Genesis 12:1–13:18.
10. See Genesis 2–3.
11. See Matthew 13:12.
12. See Matthew 25:14–28.
13. See Exodus 4:10–6:12.
14. See John 6:1–14.
15. See Philippians 3:13.
16. See 1 Corinthians 13:5.
17. See 1 Corinthians 13:7.
18. See Mark 12:29–31.
19. See John 8:1–11.

ABOUT THE AUTHOR

Victoria Osteen has always had an infectious passion and enthusiasm for life. A native Houstonian, Victoria began her career in her family's jewelry business and now works with the most precious treasure of all — people. She is an inspiration and mentor to women everywhere as she ministers alongside her husband, Joel, and sets a wonderful example for their two children, Jonathan and Alexandra. Victoria is active in her community and committed to helping women, children, and families discover their purpose and reach their highest potential.

Visit the Osteen website at www.joel osteen.com.

The employees of Thorndike Press hope you have enjoyed this Large Print book. All our Thorndike, Wheeler, and Kennebec Large Print titles are designed for easy reading, and all our books are made to last. Other Thorndike Press Large Print books are available at your library, through selected bookstores, or directly from us.

For information about titles, please call:
(800) 223-1244

or visit our Web site at:
http://gale.cengage.com/thorndike

To share your comments, please write:
Publisher
Thorndike Press
295 Kennedy Memorial Drive
Waterville, ME 04901